Ancestors

JOHN AWEN

Green Magic

Green Magic
53 Brooks Road
Street
Somerset
BA16 0PP
England

www.greenmagicpublishing.com

Designed & typeset by
K.DESIGN, Winscombe, Somerset

ISBN 9780995547810

GREEN MAGIC

Contents

Acknowledgements

WRITING THIS BOOK has been an amazing journey, right from the idea of it, then the subsequent collection of information notes and the penning of it. It has been a truly remarkable journey that has bought me much closer to not only my ancestors and lineage, but also to the collective ancestry as a whole.

I have thoroughly enjoyed writing this and as with any subject we have passions about, with that we also need comforts which make the journey much more pleasurable and enjoyable. Along with the comforts of food and drink needed to fuel our imaginations while undertaking any task, the inspirations we can gain from often overlooked comforts can really push us forward. These comforts for me are having the safe and secure place in which to feel at ease enough to write in the first place, something often overlooked and taken for granted by many.

Many thanks to those who have taken the time to offer, and give me, their advice and understanding of this subject, which is great and always stimulates the mind and helps achieve new ideas and understandings.

To my close friends and confidants who have sat drinking coffee with me when all I could talk about was this book and its creation. Friends who have made me smile and picked me up when I felt I had writers block and couldn't find the words. Many thanks to my best friend Pagan, my Black Labrador dog who has lain at my feet constantly, yet has also reminded me that it's time to venture out and go for a walk and enjoy that special time within the great outdoors amongst the elements and nature.

Huge thanks to my publisher, friend and apparent mentor Pete, who has taken the time and energy to chat and listen to me when I could not find the right formula for this book and my words were simply not flowing freely and at times were obscure in the first couple of drafts. Cheers Pete, many thanks to you.

I could not leave out all of my ancestors, without who there would be no book at all. They have gifted me this life and it is with fond and treasured memories that I have received the inspiration to research and consequently write all of the words contained within these pages, thank you to you all and I am truly humbled by what you have all gone through, endured and overcome and in doing so have gifted me the life I have today.

In memory of my Mum and Dad. Thank you for everything you showed and taught me, your careful nurturing and love of me. I love you and there is not a single day that passes where I do not think of either of you and remember you both fondly.

Preface

FROM THE FRAGILE, delicate and humble beginnings that saw the birthing of the universe and the world as we now know it, humans have emerged, slowly at first, unsure of their surroundings, timid, vulnerable and naïve. Through the mists of time we have steadily and surely reached this point now and if we care to gaze back through the aeons, right back over millennia and over the millions of years since the first birthing, we can see, sense and feel the spirits of old, those precious souls who have toiled, crafted, moulded and seeded our very essence along the way, delivering us all and allowing our life force to come into action. All of these beings, who have walked the lands, have gone before and are now passed, are our ancestors.

Much of where we have come from is shrouded in mystery, cloaked by the fabric of time, still woven intricately though and each strand carefully stitched to make up the bigger picture of our lineage, our heritage and standing there resolute against the harsh ethereal winds as a mark of testimony, strength, resolution and sheer grit, often in the face of adversity and against the odds. To reflect, ponder and gaze upon where we have come from is truly awe inspiring and totally humbling. Every soul and being that has walked before has had a part to play, however distant they may seem, in crafting the way for all of us to be living here and now.

From these small, tender and primitive beginnings, mankind has pushed on and taken our place within the world. Many beings have lived since the dawn of creation and every single one of them has had a part to play, an intrinsic and fundamental piece of our jigsaw that is our heritage, our lineage, our history and our ancestry.

Slowly, surely and steadily, the web of life in human form has been spun, now covering all areas of this beautiful planet which we call home. It is a testimony that has endured and shows the sheer resilience of mankind as a species. Whether we are aware of who our ancestors are, they all stand there and form the basis of whom we are and how we came into being. From the photographs we have in family albums, which provide us with a direct link to our closest and most recent family members, back further to names that we may have heard on a whisper as a distant relative, way back through time, we are all connected and all of these beings are our Ancestors.

In today's way of life, tracing our ancestry and lineage has never been easier and more accessible. A truly fascinating subject and an infinite journey which if we choose to start, will more than likely become very addictive and remarkable, as we slowly peel away the years and reveal many, many characters that have all had a say and an active part in delivering us to where and who we are now.

Without even looking, I know from family documents and books, that my Granddad on my Dad's side was wounded in 1916 in the first battle of the Somme during the First World War. He was injured by shrapnel which entered his lower leg, effectively rendering him unfit for service. It is with great pride that I still have that piece of shrapnel, which was removed in 1939 after it worked its way out naturally from his upper leg, some 23 years later.

One fascinating great Uncle of mine was a Baptist preacher. Charles Haddon Spurgeon was also a prolific author and in his day also preached to several thousand people at Crystal Palace in London, which was quite something back in the 1850's and to have had several thousand people attend to listen to him then, is remarkable. I would like to think that it is from him that I get my passion for the written word and writing as a whole, it would be nice to think so, effectively carrying on a family trait.

The journey of delving into the archives is indeed a magical look into where we have come from and can show us who and what we are all made up of. A vast array and a mass of invisible fingerprints, imbuing us with our bloodline, our looks, our features, certain mannerisms and our eccentricities, which we all have. Some of these features may be prominent, some are slightly more obscure, even forgotten maybe, but it is all of these personal quirks that make us exactly who we are and as we lift the lid onto our Ancestry, we can maybe reveal where these pieces of our very own and personal jigsaw have derived from.

We are all on a personal journey in this life, we each face our own fates, our own destinies and we each aspire and wish to reach our own goals and dreams, all of these may not be unique, it's the way we face them and how we reach them that makes them all personal and special to us. This matters if we start to carefully unwrap and explore our past, therefore acknowledging where we have come from. No two peoples arrival at this point in time is the same, we are each made up of a totally unique series of events, however small they may seem, without one piece of our own personal jigsaw, the picture fails and we would and could not be here right now, doing what we do and living the very life we enjoy.

Like opening up the proverbial Pandora's Box, that box contains everyone who has played a part in our own history, therefore they have also gifted and granted us our future at the same time. Small sparks emanating from the very dawn of time, slowly gaining more energy and power which in turn, generates more sparks and so on. Slowly but surely, our lineage was being built up, this can inevitably provide us all with focus points and give us areas and Ancestors to look back upon, delve into and build the picture which encompasses all the souls and beings that created us and gifted us all with that spark of life.

Reflecting and probing into our lineage is a voyage of discovery unlike any other. A truly personal journey where we can become totally absorbed both by the delights we find and also by the tragedies we may encounter, which some of our ancestors would have endured and gone through.

We may feel total kinship and resonate with many of these beings on the journey, or we may not. There could be one special relative that we feel closer to than others, maybe we look like them, have a similar career, likes, dislikes, views, who knows? What will inevitably happen, is that we will bring these people to life in a sense, albeit momentarily, we will be discovering and remembering them, paying homage and honouring those who have helped stitch and weave the very fabric of our life, as we lift the lid and look back upon their lives, who they were and what part they played in creating us and gifting us our personal lives now.

An infinite number of people who have lived before and are now passed, some forgotten in the mists of time, some more recognisable and prominent, have all had their part to play and have each carefully woven a strand into the tapestry which is the picture of our life and if we cast our minds back and look, we can see the very same tapestry is their picture as well.

However we each choose to view the past, our past, we cannot fail to recognise the significance when bought together as a whole, the total and unforeseen forces along with beings, that have seeded along the way, the trail of lives gone, circumstances unseen and the universal forces which have transpired into a cataclysmic series and mind boggling sequence of events to quite simply pave the way for us to be standing here now.

To metaphorically speak, it is easier now than ever to connect with our ancestors simply by searching on line and this provides us with great insight and an opening pivotal point to find out who they were. Metaphysically speaking, we can then lift the veil between worlds within ourselves and call upon them for many answers and any guidance which we seek, or feel we might need.

Whichever way we decide or comfortably opt to bring these souls to life by discovering them and therefore connecting with them, we are allowing their lives and deeds to flow through us, which will grant us a deeper connection and understanding of them all.

I hope you enjoy this book and the alternative journey which I will take you on within these pages.

If you would like to contact me personally, about this book, or other books I have written, please feel free to do so via my website www.johnawen.com.

Within and around us Constantly

AS EACH ONE of us stands here, we form part of a complete picture. Within ourselves as people, we are whole, whereas the pictures we are a part go way back through the mists of time. Each breath we take, every footstep we tread and every single heartbeat that drives us on, is steeped and impregnated with the very essence of our ancestors and those who have gone before us, paving the way for us all to be here now.

The ancestors, our ancestors all form part of an infinite and unseen universal web of mystery, some we have seen, or heard of, many though have not been recorded to view, but still stand there a very complex part of who we are and even though we do not know their names, or faces, we must remember and honour them all.

Kaleidoscopic arrays of immeasurable parts, paths and people have lived, worked and passed on, culminating in an incalculable number of lives which make us the people we are today. Bathed in the DNA of millions of individual souls and beings, it is these people that we need to recognise, give thanks and pay homage to, because without them, our lives as we know it, would simply pale into insignificance and we would not exist in the form which we do now.

Etched and scribed into the mirrors of the ages and all that has passed before, these Ancestors stand and are now reflecting themselves into us and through us. We do not stand as just ourselves, alone, we may be individuals, but our very individuality is only here because of the vast array of souls, their blood, bone, characteristics and traits, basically their very imprint which we carry within us. This is not necessarily just harnessed within us, but is all around us also and in all we do. Their spirits are in the air we inhale, within the very ground and earth which we tread upon and contained for all of time, held tightly in the universe.

Imagine if you can, the most intricate puzzle, with countless layers of such depth, which are almost impossible to comprehend. Since the very birth of creation, human beings have been on a course of evolution, growing in strength, gaining numbers constantly, pushing all the boundaries of intellect, physique, bodily structure, multiple and diversified languages and a plethora of other incredible traits and prowess, delivering us to this point in time and arriving with each and every one of us as we stand here today in our mortal existence.

Now try to perceive that our very being is spliced from, holds and contains the very essence and make up of all these beings that have lived and gone before us. Layer upon layer of human DNA is contained within all of us. From the relatively recent discovery of a small Hominid being, affectionately named 'Lucy', who has been dated as living on this planet over 3 million years ago, right through to our very own Mothers and Fathers, we consist of all of these beings, however remotely it may be, we carry all of humanity within us to some degree.

It may seem impossible to imagine, but if we could lift the shrouds that separate our world from the world of our ancestors, we would see such a diversified group of people and beings that stand there as a test of time and so many other attributes, all helping mankind as a whole to move forward, cogs in a wheel basically, turning constantly and evolving on all levels with each new generation that has lived and breathed. Growing, spreading, evolving, shifting and moving through the time frame and scale as we now know and comprehend it. A huge sweeping mass of individual souls, that when combined with each other form an immeasurable amount of life force and various energies. It is this colossal life force that slowly and surely set out and has made the journey through time and age to arrive in the here and now as we all stand here in the present as testimony to this.

Undeniably, it is a mass fusion and combination of all these individuals that is enveloped within every single one of us. Not so hard to imagine really, often extremely hard to comprehend fully, but to appreciate the now and the lives we have and live, we cannot overlook this miraculous arrival to this moment in time without at least trying to perceive the great and distinguished lineage that we are all imbued with and carry inside us constantly.

As we live our lives', we are all effectively living for those who have passed on, as we are carrying their genes and very make up accordingly deep within us. Yes they no longer physically exist in a sense of having their own human bodies and walking this earthly realm, it is within us that they live now, as without any of these precious individuals, our very existence would not be.

Our Ancestors are within and around us constantly. They may have lived thousands, some even millions of years ago; we must never let that detract from the fact that they have all played a part in our very creation and mere existence. However distant and unrecognisable, even obscure, they may seem, like the links in a chain, each one is as vital and important as the next one. Take one link out, the chain fails and if the chain breaks, well, sure you can see my analogy in this?

13

From the precious stirrings of creation right through to the birthing and dawn of each new day that we see and witness, we are watching, absorbing and playing a part in the evolution of mankind. Every new day heralds a new start and as we watch this amazing natural wonder unfold, we are witness to what each one of our ancestors has gazed upon and absorbed since time first began. Not only are we voyeurs to all we see for ourselves, we are playing out and taking it all in for each one of those beings who have gone before us, all paving the way and weaving the constant thread of life, creation and guiding us on our journey into and through each day.

As we wake each morning and marvel at the world, the sights, smells, sounds, feelings, sensations and all that is contained within this beautiful and immense world and universe, we must show respect, give honour and gratitude for all that there is, all that we have and are and pay homage to the Ancestors, for it is their perseverance, strengths, sacrifices and endurance that has delivered us into being, granting and enabling us to be here now. We are them as they are us and they are within and around us constantly and in all we do.

What is an Ancestor?

THIS IS A question that has several variations, albeit fairly similar. In a nutshell, the widely appreciated meaning of the word and noun ancestor is: Any person from whom one is descended.

If we look at this a bit more in depth and I will use the easily recognisable metaphor of a family tree, as we can all relate to this and also when using this, it is commonly known the world over, when looking into and discovering your ancestry, you are effectively delving into the archives of a family tree.

Basically while undertaking this journey into lineage and genealogy, we invariably start with our own parents. Liken this path of discovery to the newest and freshest top branches on the tree. From this new emergence and growth, the journey can and will ultimately take us further into the tree. Along and through old and solid branches and boughs and if we could venture far enough into this tree, we would slowly be guided and shown who and what makes up the solid trunk of the tree and then invariably, highly unlikely and almost impossible for now, we could journey into the very soil and explore the root system which has provided us with the very life force and essence which birthed creation to start with.

The records which are slowly building nowadays, are providing us with the tools to go back further and further, unfortunately I don't think that we will ever be able to physically discover quite where and who we have all derived from, in any case, the one life we have now could not grant us enough time to undertake this series of infinite findings and exploring.

Each new generation provides and gifts us beautiful new lush foliage to the ever growing tree of ancestry and for anybody that has ever started to look into their past, they will know how totally absorbing, fascinating and addictive this can be.

It is not unheard of for some people to have traced their own ancestry back almost one thousand years, which is amazing. Depending on how these people lived, social classing of the day, places they lived, areas and countries all depend on how easy, or how difficult delving into and building up our family tree can be. It should be easy enough with all the modern resources there are available to us nowadays, to trace back, without any real problems, somewhere between 300–500 years. Take into account how many people are involved in this and even this relatively short space of time is a major undertaking and should satisfy anybody who decides to delve and explore their lineage.

Once we decide to look into our pasts, every person and relative we encounter and find, is obviously one of our ancestors and this can build up an incredible picture that effectively is bringing the past to life, these souls into being and giving us a much more intimate sense of who we are as we discover our own heritage and the chain of evolution that has worked throughout time to bring us to this exact point now, along with many individuals who were personally involved in this infinite and timeless process.

To digress a bit and to speak hyperbole, it is not too farfetched to see ourselves as our own ancestors. If we look at past lives for instance, that we may, or may not have lived, then it is plausible that we are then related to ourselves, therefore we have been part and parcel of forming and weaving our own strands of heritage and lineage, which if we think about that in an abstract way, then the evidence becomes very acceptable.

It is widely estimated that since mankind first arrived on Earth and to date, there have been 107 billion people that have lived, breathed and existed. This is an estimate, but I can't think of any reason why it is not far from the truth. With 7 billion individuals alive at this time, the maths behind this shows us that for each person alive now, then another 15 people have lived and died. When we think about that, admittedly the sheer numbers are mind blowing and quite surreal really, but if we for a moment think that we have all trod this Earth, then surely we are all connected.

We are all children of this Earth. We are all made from the same seeds and made up of similar particles. We have pretty much the same blood flowing through our veins. The life force of air that we all inhale to live is the same, as are many of our traits and we basically function in the same, or very comparable ways, so we are not too far removed from one another then, are we?

Directly, or indirectly, we all share the same origins, albeit way back in the mists of time. Undeniably we were all originally seeded from the same lineage, it's just from that point of origin, many different factions, matriarchs and patriarchs have all had their part to play, which as the population grew and grew, the DNA structure and various genes which provide our base make up have changed, altering with each new strand that arrives, therefore furthering our dilution from our original source and point of conception. This is how we can invariably see, understand and grasp, that we are not that far removed from one another. This is just another take, a rather large take admittedly, on the tree of Ancestry. If we imagine that we can go as far back as the basic and main root structure, it will show us we all arrive from the same root system, which begs the answer, we are all connected.

Obviously nowadays, it is acceptable to over look the fact that we all source and originate from the same place. A very complex and extremely diversified practice which on paper, would be almost impossible to trace and link together. We now concentrate and view our own lineage and Ancestry with relative ease and accessibility, which basically shows us our own unique tribe, community and how we have all evolved and culminated through the years and over the generations that have gone before us.

An ancestor therefore is a being in which we have descended from, our direct bloodline incorporating our Mothers and Fathers sides and slowly budding out from these two beings. Souls and precious individuals who have come together on their journey through life, which has bought into being new souls, eventually once again creating more new souls and so the vast array of connectivity carries on and the more branches of our family tree which we discover, then the more branches we uncover and so this amazing investigation into our lineage and genetic makeup continues, basically the more we look, the more we invariably find. An incredible parting of the mists of time happens when not only do we look into what is an Ancestor? But more to the point, who are our ancestors?

Honouring our Ancestors

THERE ARE AN infinite number of ways, variations and interpretations as to how we can honour our ancestors. As with many different parts of life, there are ways that we can follow to do this, just with putting our own stamp on them, personalising them in as to what and how suits us, our position at that time and what feels comfortable to us as we do this.

From the first stirrings of the universe and creation as a whole, mankind has observed all there is around, from the dawn of each new day and the first light, to the abundant new growth in the fields, trees and hedgerows. Birds flying overhead, soaring in the skies above, through to the vast amount of wildlife and various creatures that adorn our planet and environments, all of this has been gazed upon, perused over and appreciated since mankind first arrived on this planet. The sun, moon and all the planets and alignments within our solar system have bought peace, tranquillity, wonderment, awe, solace, inspiration and a plethora of other thoughts, aspirations and ideas to all of mankind before us. As we view and savour all these sights, we are merely partaking in all the majestic and splendid variety of natural gifts and blessings which our ancestors have enjoyed before us. To acknowledge and enjoy all this bounty, is undoubtedly a way in which we totally connect with the universe and in doing so, we connect and give Honour to those who have now passed.

From mountain tops, undulating hills, meandering natural springs and rivers, arid deserts, lakes, swamps, the list goes on and on, it is within all this rich natural beauty that millions of people before us, our lineage and ancestry have sought peace, taken refuge and shelter, bathed, walked, shed tears, sweat and bled. Their past is stained, etched and echoes out to us from and through the very same places we live, walk and visit. Forever held within the lands as a constant mirror reflecting outwards to us to hold them dear, remember fondly and Honour them in all we do and undertake.

It is no coincidence, as I don't believe in them, merely synchronicities that I am writing this in 2016. One hundred years ago saw the Battle of the Somme start, which still to this day is the bloodiest battle known to man. A battle within the First World War (1914–1918) and one my Granddad fought in and was subsequently injured. Many people alive today will no doubt have a relative, more than likely passed on by now, who fought in this War, or at least the Second World War, (1939–1945) showing us within our lives that our recent Ancestors fought and shed blood on the lands we live in and around, or can visit.

The way we live our lives is held, captured for time within the ether and is cradled there for all of eternity. Not one person is ever lost and forgotten and neither has any life ever been lived and endured for no reason, all of these precious and sacred souls are merely held there for us all to remember, connect with and give Honour to.

The dead cannot speak, yet if we tune in, we can hear their whispers, sense the messages they offer and appreciate their guidance and wisdom. They have lived their lives, often in the face of adversity, pains, trauma, yet they have left us with a legacy and our voices to Honour them with and remember them fondly, often and in all we do and undertake.

Quiet contemplation when we first awake at the dawning of a new day is a great way to pay and give Honour to our Ancestors. In this still and undisturbed time, we can reflect and ponder on those who have passed and gone before us. This stillness resonates deep within us and as well as being extremely cathartic and an ideal way to start the day, we are embracing the almost meditative and tranquil state before the start of each day that has been appreciated by all those who have lived before. As if the veil lifts between worlds momentarily, this quiet time can see us cradled and nestled within the very bosom of our departed ancestors.

Throughout our journey of each day, those who we have loved and have gifted us life, are merely a whisper and a heartbeat away. No walls or doors separate us, just our own structured and regimented lifestyles, which in today's modern society is unfortunately par for the course. It is even more imperative nowadays to make time for quiet reflection, meditation and alone time. It is within these moments that our human conditioning can be released and let go of, when this happens and we acquire the willingness and state of consciousness to allow this to happen, we slip into an almost natural and trance like state of mind, from this we connect and tap into the natural source of creation and the universe as a whole. Once reached, we can then let go and find inner solace, peace and a more attuned level of being. From this point, we can metaphysically travel wherever we like and in doing this, we are guided and watched over by our ancient loved ones, who in turn can provide us with total inner peace, calmness, answers we may be seeking, clarity, inner wisdom and a whole host of other natural and very much needed spiritual guidance.

For our recently deceased ancestors, parents, grandparents, uncles and aunties, we can easily focus on their birthdays and dates of when they passed away. These provide an intimate and specific time in which to remember them. On these dates, we can hold them fondly in our hearts and in our minds, which effectively grants them life again as while we remember these souls that have enriched our lives; they are still alive within us. The modern technology we have today is incredible as we can easily and quickly take high quality photographs often without the subject being aware we have captured them on camera. These photographs can gift us much comfort and are an amazing way of viewing, seeing and sensing that person even when they have ceased to be.

Presents they may have given us, cards which have been sent, photographs, written letters and their personal effects are all great in providing us with the essence of that person and these pieces are always a lovely reminder of the life they lived and shared with us. Echoing and calling to us from beyond the veil, these material items remind us each day, especially if we have their photographs on display, that they are not really gone, they are still within and around us constantly and all of these items and deeds are very valuable and personalised ways of honouring our ancestors.

Candles are lit and are used in most religions, across many cultures and are used in a multitude of varying traditions around the world as a way of signifying and symbolising loved ones. Fire is well known as, among many other attributes and powers, it can bring clarity, a focal point and is a great representation to see, feel and sense a connection to our dearly departed and much missed loved ones and ancestors. To light a candle and to watch the delicate flame flicker and dance is probably the most widely used and respected portrayal of our deceased that we have and use and it is commonplace throughout most of the modern world as a way of connecting with those departed souls that we miss and hold dear to us.

From the moment we first awake and say our quiet invocations to the universe, we are tapping into and giving thanks not only for our life, but also for the lives of our ancestors who have ensured our delivery to this point in time. Make no mistake, however we manifest our hopes, dreams and aspirations, they are heard and transmitted to those they are supposed to reach. An infinite lineage is lined up behind and around us, listening, and hearing, supporting and guiding us from beyond the veil. It is these words, whether whispered, silently thought, or vocalised that are a perfect way of giving thanks and honouring those passed. All the souls who have now passed, lived their lives as they did, effectively becoming vessels to bring us to who and where we are now. If we reverse that, we can see that the baton has now been passed to us and it is each one of us that stands here now living our lives, not just for us, but for every being that has ever had and played a part in delivering us to this point in time and granting us this beautiful life that we each now lead.

The very lives we have and live nowadays are so enriched and it is from the sheer determination, often sacrifices from those gone before us, that has ensured that we can now live as freely and as openly as we do. Everything is on offer to us and so readily available. The freedom we often take for granted, freedom to travel, of speech, to pursue our careers, the list is endless. We now live in the most accessible of times ever, on all of our levels, both physically and metaphysically and all of this has been achieved and stands as testimony to every single one of the ancestors, whether they are our direct lineage or not.

These precious souls and beings have paved the way and still stand there resolutely, albeit it in a different form now, for us to connect with, hold dear, remember fondly and give honour and respect to whenever we can.

From the mementoes we keep and the photographs we display of our loved and departed family members, through to the bunches of flowers and floral tributes that we lay on a grave, or in a garden of remembrance, all of these actions, however small and insignificant they may seem, or appear, are all ways in which we can personally give thanks to the deceased and in doing this, we keep their spirit and very essence alive.

Many cultures around the world have designated days and periods of time where the dead are celebrated and reverence is shown totally. Within the Celtic wheel of the year, Samhain, which in the Northern Hemisphere is on 31st October, is the date when Pagans, Wiccans, Celts, Neo – Pagans and several other beliefs and paths, honour their deceased and departed loved ones, friends and Ancestors. It is widely acknowledged that at this time, the veil that separates our world from theirs, is almost non – existent, therefore providing a perfect time to communicate and honour the departed.

Mexico is a country that is renowned for its celebrations on this date and in their culture and many Hispanic countries and communities, it is called 'Dia de los Muertos,' or Day of the Dead. This very elaborate, spectacular and inspirational celebration of the deceased is now celebrated across much of the U.S. An almost carnival like atmosphere is created within larger towns during this celebration, costumes are worn by many, food and drink is readily available and on offer and altars are erected as another form of symbolism to give thanks and to honour the dead and departed. Beliefs behind this stem from the notion that at midnight on the 31st October each year, the gates of heaven open up, thus allowing the deceased and living to be united once again. This very sacred and wonderful celebration of lives now gone has its roots way back in history and the celebration can be traced back to around 3,000 years ago, when it was originally started by the Aztecs.

There are many countries and cultures that celebrate the dead and it is vital and essential to continue these timeless traditions and in doing so, they are showing total respect, giving thanks and honour to all those who have walked these lands before and who are now sadly departed.

I personally find it comforting that so many tribes and cultures not only remember their dead, but they totally celebrate their departed family members, loved ones and ancestors in general. Once we show respect and give thanks in celebrations, however small or large they may be, we are letting our deceased know that their lives have not been forgotten and they will continue to be remembered for all of time. In doing this, we gift them and effectively bestow life force upon and within them, simply because every action we undertake or partake in within this life, is echoed through the veil and is felt in other worlds and realms in which these precious souls now exist and are at peace.

There are small actions which we can each do, if we choose, on a daily basis to remember our loved ones. From gazing up at the skies above as our ancestors have done since time began. We can smile fondly at their memory; whisper a name to the wind, display a photograph, visit a grave, it is all these small tokens and gestures that keep us connected and in touch with those who we love and have parted now from this world. On a larger scale, red poppies are worn by millions of people to remember all those who have tragically lost their lives during war time. As I mentioned, large celebrations are held in many countries around the world and have been for many years. The significance and symbolism to these events is to show that the dead are and will be remembered and that their lives are respected, appreciated and totally honoured, as they should be.

However we personally remember and show respect to those who have passed, doesn't matter, it's the very fact that we do that counts. Whether we give thanks quietly and alone, or whether we choose to join in with larger groups and attend organised events and celebrations, it is totally down to us as individuals and is our personal choice. The connections and honour we have and show will be felt by those that it is intended for, regardless. So long as we do give respect, honour and remember all those who have led us to this point, therefore granting us this wonderfully enriched life we now live, that is what truly matters.

Echoes of Time

AS WE WALK upon this sacred earth, the memories and lingering essence of our departed loved ones and ancestors, is around us in all we see, imprinted upon and within the most ordinary of everyday items and sights. Many seemingly regular and common personal thoughts and memories, along with more physical items are a constant reminder that we are not alone and never will be. Whether we choose to acknowledge and see them as reflections of cherished memories of loved ones, or maybe we almost take these imprints of the past for granted, what is important, is that if we realise how much of our modern society and lifestyles have been shaped, moulded and have evolved from all those who have gone before, then it becomes much clearer to identify with and know what a massive part all of these sacred souls have played in helping us to reach this point in time, and enjoy life as we do.

Our families which we physically have are a constant reminder to us of members who have passed on, a surviving family member may often recall a memory they have and then we can all smile with melancholic reflection, warming those who are still alive, a small and significant way of remembering that person fondly, and carrying that cherished memory within our hearts.

Favourite places are a great way to remember, we may have visited them with someone who has now gone on, or they may have talked about wanting to visit. This can at times, unknowingly, become like a pilgrimage. I have been to places before and then been reminded in my mind, that my Mum, or Dad spoke about visiting, and then never did for whatever reason. This then warms me immensely as it is if I am seeing the sights and taking it all in, not just for myself, but for them. I have smiled several times when this has happened, as it is undeniable as to why I am there, I can only know and recognise that I have been prompted to visit and been guided there by my own loved ones who have now departed. I have no doubt that several of you will have similar stories that you are now remembering and recollecting?

As children, we absorb, take in and follow many ideas and thinking from our parents. We may support a football, cricket, or other sporting team, merely because they did. Often this only becomes obvious once that person has ceased to be; nevertheless we carry on supporting that team, often more vehemently than we did before, as if pushed on by them, also as a mark of respect and fondness to that person.

An abundance and array of lifestyles, ideas, traits, mannerisms and how we view and associate certain aspects along with the way we act, sense and view the world can a lot of the time, be attributed to our parents and those who have played a pivotal role in our upbringing, once again, these don't always become clear, or even noticed, until we are without that person physically, it is often when coping with death and loss, that we go into recall and these seemingly mundane thoughts and feelings, come into being and make sense to us, driving us on and warming our very centre.

There is an old saying, 'we never know what we have, until it's gone,' this is so true. It is so easy to take people for granted, often without intending to we can almost be nonchalant, carefree and slightly oblivious that they are in our lives and have created us. As I am writing this, I am constantly remembering my parents and this makes me smile but also brings an inner sadness that they have both now passed away. It is vital that we cherish our loved ones and I felt at this point in this book, I just had to say, hold all your loved ones closely while you can.

The echoes of our departed loved ones and ancestors call out and reverberate to us constantly from beyond the grave, embedded for all of eternity as a constant reminder of those we love and those who have shaped and structured our very lives, even though, they are no longer with us.

Whispers on the breeze often stir, rekindle and bring to the forefront of our minds; special memories of individuals and at times, cherished people and those who we have loved. We may see a colour that they wore frequently and favoured, we might walk past a particular tree, see a flower they loved. At times we could find ourselves hearing a tune on the radio that they sung along to, a birdcall they enjoyed, we may hear their name mentioned, the list is infinite and is personalised entirely by memories that you have of that person, which is so beautiful to have and is another way of that person reaching out to us, touching our very being and making sure that these memories we have of them, will keep their spirit alive within us.

If we look now towards the more physical and touchable objects that there are around within our everyday lives, which can link us to those who have gone before, essentially providing us with a more direct and personalised way that we can touch their essence and feel them still around us.

These solid and physical artefacts, memories and personalised treasures hold extremely precious connections and the difference is, we can actually touch, handle and unite on a much deeper level, with the person who left, gifted or bequeathed them to us. They can come in a whole host of various forms, from tools, cutlery sets, vases, random ornaments, a car maybe that they owned and drove, items of furniture, the list goes on and on. These personal pieces would probably mean nothing at all to others, but to us, they are imbued with our loved ones imprint and very essence, therefore to us, they are priceless, irreplaceable and totally sentimental, giving, allowing and significantly forging the connections we had to these people, which now continues through these individual pieces, whatever they may be, to us though, they are priceless and always will be.

The links we have to our departed loved ones and ancestors knows no bounds and can often present and manifest themselves in such a wide and diversified way, that it is almost as if they are around us and within us constantly if we choose to accept, tap in and recognise this. Some people might be left the family home in a will, or as part of a legacy. This obviously can then become an undeniable and a very intimate connection to the special souls that are sadly no longer with us in the physical sense, but their very spirits and echoes are around us constantly and they are embedded totally in the very framework in which we may live.

Graveyards, crematoriums and remembrance gardens are one of the most thought about places of final rest, which is true, as these hold the final memories of many beings, as these were the last places that we paid respect, said farewell and celebrated the life that was, as we sent them on their way to the Summerlands, the resting place beyond the veil that separates our world from theirs. These sacred and hallowed places of rest are a great comfort, as they readily provide a space where we can go to connect, pay tribute to, with flowers, ornaments, candles, etc.

As human beings living in a very physical world, it is places like graveyards and other similar locations, where we can actually see a headstone, remembrance plaque, or a tree that may have been planted in their honour, which gives and allows us to know and fully be aware of that person's final resting place. All of these varying types of symbolism, in a physical form, are essential to us, as well as bestowing comfort, they also provide a conduit, a gateway, or channel that grants us access and recognised solidification to that person, or persons who have now expired and left this earthly plain.

The world around us, the communities, towns and villages which we live in and go about our daily lives are impregnated deeply with the spirits and etchings of all those who have lived there before. Going back further now, it is our ancestors, whether directly linked to and with us, that have crafted and built every single aspect which we associate, see and use on our journey through each day. The roads and pathways which we drive and walk upon, the hedgerows that grow in our gardens and fields, they have all been built, laid and planted accordingly, by our ancestors. The subways, train tracks, gardens we walk through, the pubs and shops we frequent and spend money in, all of these are timeless reminders and they all hold within and carry remnants of lives lived before, worked in, visited, toiled over and constructed by those who have lived, breathed and worked here before. Like invisible footprints slowly covered with age and history, there all the same though, and it is through these precious souls who once lived, that evolution, progress and the lives we often take for granted have been reached, achieved and granted to and for us.

Vestiges of what has been, lives that were once lived and people that once walked this earth are around us constantly and take on many forms. Constant reminders and archetypal manifestations are abundant and can be seen, felt, touched and sensed the world over. Our ancestors, whether recently departed, or those who died long ago, they have all played a part in creating the world as we know it now and it is to each and every one of these beautiful souls that we owe a great deal of gratitude, thanks and should remember fondly whenever we can. A constant and infinite lineage of forefathers and foremothers and those who we have derived from, all had their part to play in shaping and moulding us.

They Call and Reach Out to Us

FROM BEYOND THE veil, held within in a different realm, our departed and deceased loved ones, our ancestors still carry on communicating to us, just in altered ways and through various approaches. They call and reach out to us, permeating the unseen and invisible shroud that hangs between and separates our world from theirs.

There are many different openings and ways that we are communicated to from beyond the veil, often we can be oblivious to the fact that we are being spoken to by our departed loved ones, yet once we attune ourselves to what is, in effect, a different frequency if you like, then we can become more open and accepting of this communication.

Due to the fact we are living and contained within our mortal human bodies, we expect any correspondence we receive, to come to us in a physical form. Seeing as in reading, whether that is in the form of books or newspapers (and nowadays, via our laptops and phones) we absorb through our eyes, which is a major way that we take in communication. Hearing what is being said is vital as well and is another trait in which we comprehend, acknowledge and understand the world around us. These are both extremely powerful membranes that allow us to recognise a lot of what is going on around us in our day to day lives, basically letting us accept various signals and communications.

When we take into consideration that around 90% of all communication is non-verbal, then we can start sensing and feeling that we have many other channels and senses that allow us to relate to information that is being sent (or transmitted to us directly, and around us) Whatever form it may arrive to us. From this we can totally grasp that we are open conduits and we absorb a vast number of messages, symbols, facts, figures and alternative conversations, without even thinking about it.

Guidance, various messages, clarity, insights, answers and a whole host of other tidings are given to us in many forms. It is up to us whether or not we relay and respond, or even recognise these intimations when they arrive to us. Often we are so caught up with our busy day to day lives, that we totally miss these symbolic and often extremely powerful and useful messages, simply because they are being emitted to us in a way that we often fail to comprehend. As in we are not receiving them in a physical manifestation. So we then tend to overlook, or dismiss them totally, which is a shame. All of us ask for guidance, it depends on whether or not we form it in our minds, or vocalise it to the universe, as to our comprehension and acknowledgement that we are actually asking for answers to begin with. Once we realise this, then we become so much more open and susceptible that the questions we are asking, will get answered, often just not in the same sense, or way in which our physical self is accustomed to.

When we sleep, we are basically in a limbo-type stasis, our physical selves have switched off to recharge and rest and our minds take over to sort out our mental self, effectively reordering what we need to focus on and ejecting thoughts we don't necessarily need. This dream state that we are in allows messages to flow in to us. If we truly need to comprehend a message then we are often able to remember the dream upon waking. This state of physical unawareness, allows us to be heightened and responsive in our subconscious forms, therefore allowing any guidance we have asked for, or need, to freely flow through and remain with us once we wake.

I have no doubt at all, that at some point, we have all had dreams that stay with us and feature a loved one, a friend, or a person that we recognise, yet we know full well that they have departed this world, or maybe they do shortly afterwards? These dreams are some of the most powerful and expressive types we can have, as it is our loved ones and ancestors who are delivering them to us. We trusted and loved these souls while they were alive, now they are sadly passed, it is even more vital and imperative that we listen to, and heed the messages and signs that they show and bring to us.

The dead are not so far away; they are with us and around us constantly and in all we do. The veil that separates us, is a permeable membrane, we can visit them and vice versa, allowing an exchange, guidance and answers to be passed. More often than not, it is these loved ancestors who make the transition into our world, to offer hope, strength, love and comfort to us, often when we most need it.

Smells are a reminder that those we knew, who have now passed, are close by. It could be a faint odour of perfume which we can relate to and feel a departed loved one by. Fragrances and familiar smells transport us back in time in an instant, they hold a great significance and representation of times gone by, and people in particular. Permeating the veil from beyond the grave, a slight, or at times almost overpowering aroma, can instantly resonate within us and we can then sense, feel and know that we are not alone. A loved family member or special friend is visiting, accompanying and standing with us, just not in a physical form, but there with us all the same.

Both my parents are now passed on, I do still sense them around me quite often, urging me on and answering questions that I may have been subconsciously asking, giving me answers and clarity, always at the right time and when I need it the most. I dream about both my parents occasionally as well. When this happens I always remember the dream, as it is always powerful and intuitive advice I am being gifted by them, which obviously warms my heart and encourages me greatly. Not so often, but every now and then, I might get a faint aroma of Musk perfume, or Yardley lavender talcum powder (which were my Mum's favourite) and seeing as this happens when there is nobody else around, I know instantly that my Mum is visiting this realm and has decided to make the transition from beyond the veil, just to come and let me know that she is still with me. Occasionally I might get the unmistakeable aroma of a distinctive pipe tobacco which I remember my Dad smoked when I was a child. Another great reminder that, even though he died in 2007, he is not that far away and still visits from time to time.

To recognise these other worldly visitors and ancestors when they make themselves known and appear to us, through whichever conduit, or medium they decide to manifest, is such a gift and a very rich blessing indeed. We knew, loved and respected these souls while they lived and we looked up to them, it is no different now, just the way they communicate to and with us has changed. Once we attune and accept that they are still a part of our lives and always will be, we then let them in and the signs and messages they can show and bring to us, can not only help us immensely, but also enrich our lives and warm our hearts.

The loved ones that we shared our lives and special times

with can, and invariably do, call out, reach out and support us in our physical lives. We only have to recall all those times when we heard them call our names, even though we often tend to dismiss this as hearing voices that we could not possibly have heard. The soothing and loving hand of support we thought we felt on our shoulder, maybe even the sense of being restrained when a dangerous situation looked and seemed imminent and impossible to avoid. Maybe singing along to a song that was their favourite, enjoying a bar of chocolate which we never buy, thinking about it though, we remember it was enjoyed by a departed loved one. All of these could be put down as, and are often seen as coincidences, which I personally don't believe in, only synchronicities. However we view, sense and accept these symbols, aromas, voices and messages, which we know are other worldly, we cannot escape or deny that we have all had a similar experience. It is up to each one of us as individuals to believe what we want to and that which resonates deep within us. To deny these feelings and experiences is almost to deny they lived in the first place, which we can't do. Just because they are no longer in a physical sense and form, that does not mean they are no longer with us. All of these special, sacred and departed loved ones and ancestors are still within and around us, in all we do and undertake and they call out and reach out to us constantly. Watching with immense pride, joy, love and there to guide, help and support us. Ask them for help, they know because they have all of life's experience to call on and share with us. Open up, accept they are there and allow all the messages and signs they have to freely flow into you, heed the lessons and hold these souls within your heart, remembering them fondly and often.

Time Loop Continuum

PLAYING OUT AROUND us constantly is an inaudible and for the majority of us, unseen, recording and loop which is known as and referred to as the 'time loop continuum'. Etched and recorded from the past and playing out continuously, we are walking through parts and some of it every single day of our lives.

Unheard echoes and unseen shadows from lives that are now extinct, some ceased to be and expired thousands of years ago, yet still the residual energy they left behind goes on, a constant reminder of times gone by and of lives that once lived, yet still they linger, at work, in the homes they once had, celebrating much like we do today, generally living and enjoying their lives.

A permanent time capsule containing and replaying the energies and traces of every being that has ever lived, breathed and walked upon this beautiful planet. Their mortal and fleshy bodies have long since decayed, yet the memories live on and are playing out around us, permanently traced into the surroundings they once knew, were familiar with and which they loved, lived in and were a part of.

To make a comparison, we have all heard of ghosts, entities that manage to often make themselves relatively visible to some people and maybe even at different, sometimes certain and relative times of the day, night, or even on select days during our calendar year. To take this one step further and explain in more detail, imagine that every village, town, hamlet, thriving and bustling community that has ever been inhabited, is there in front of you now, obscured obviously, but like a carbon copy. These places are still there, we just don't necessarily see them constantly and not always with our physical eyesight. Layer upon layer of towns that once stood, altering over the years and as time moved on, growing, expanding and evolving constantly.

If we take a piece of paper and draw on it, then rub it out and draw another picture on the same paper, there remains an outline of the original sketch and the more we do this, then more remains are left, fragmented and not easily visible, but still there though. Now imagine that in the natural world that we live in today and are a part of. Time may well erase, almost eradicate some parts of our history and so much of it still lays undiscovered to this day. Yet we can feel, sense and possibly at times see our living history, although it's veiled by time, yet still it remains there, held almost in a stasis like form, playing out much like we live and go about our lives today.

Our much loved yet departed family members and our ancestors are always within and around us. The realm they now live and reside in has changed; still they exist and live out parts of their lives as they once did while they walked this earth. The remnants and energies they left behind are still around us constantly and always will be. Recorded within the ether and still playing out, this analogy could cast some light on the various hot and cold spots which we all tend to feel from time to time in different places, from our homes to places we may well visit.

As this universal and constant recording plays out around us, just hidden from sight, we still walk through these ancient rubbings of time. For the most part of it, there is nothing adverse happening, normal day to day life and the relatively mundane everyday tasks so to speak, so we tend not to feel our ancestors around us at all times. If we enter anywhere at a time of festivities, joyous celebrations, maybe the time when a baby was being born, a marriage happening, a party and so on, then we may well feel incredibly warm, the hairs may go up on the back of our necks, it is at these special times and at that moment when we cross over into the recordings of the past and can more easily feel and sense the joy that was once created, shared and celebrated there by our ancient loved ones and ancestors.

There are places which we may visit and feel drawn to and places which resonate out to us, effectively calling us there. Often we cannot explain what the pull is, we just know and accept that these particular places make us feel happy, content and almost cradle us at the times when we need it most. These could well be favoured places by our Ancestors and now they are passing on to us, the living, the joyful and blissful times they had and enjoyed while they were alive.

I personally have many specific areas and special places that call out to me, which I visit as often as I can when at all possible. Sacred places where I can stroll maybe, or just sit for hours, reflecting and contemplating on what has been and is to come. We all have favourite places and personal spaces which we enjoy visiting and spending time in and I like to think that it is these special places that have been enjoyed by our deceased loved ones and ancestors.

Over the years I have walked through, visited and driven through places that have a totally oppressive and almost unexplainable darkness around them, which I can't quite put my finger on, I just tend to avoid them and don't visit them. This could be the phenomena which are sometimes referred to as cold spots. Maybe something negative happened there, a death, murder or a full scale battle ensued there and if we visit while these are being played out within the time loop continuum, then undoubtedly we are going to pick up, sense and absorb the residual energies that are recorded and play out there at certain times.

Like permanent stains, or smudges that exist, woven into the infinite tapestry of our history and the landscapes around. Whether these are beautiful and joyous times of celebration, or whether they might be a bit more brutal, even horrific in some cases, these fragmented memories and ancient recordings of times and lives now past, are always there and will remain constantly.

Our ancient ancestors lived much as we do today, obviously without all the modern technology and transport which we have and enjoy now, but their lives on the whole were not so different, just simpler in some ways. They would have eaten, drunk, worked and toiled, they would have celebrated special events, walked within nature, married, had children and they would have also quarrelled amongst one another, often resulting in full scale fighting and/or serious battles, which is the same as we do now. All of these memories, distant artefacts and remnants of their lives and our history, may seem removed and irrelevant to us now, but once we become attuned to the various energies that are around us every day, we can at times and invariably do, pick up and sense it all. Often we fail to totally grasp and comprehend what it is we are feeling, but it is the lives and existence of these now departed loved ones and our ancestors that we are sensing and being receptive to, in the many forms that this comes to and is shown to us.

The Gradual Process of Evolution and Arrival of Human Type Beings

EVOLUTION IS A very slow and drawn out process, it has to be. When we look at our own development across time, what has happened in effect, is the very gradual arrival of ourselves, the most intelligent and diverse beings on this planet.

Approximately 55 million years ago, discoveries, studies and scientific based finds and painstaking research conducted over recent decades show us that the very first primitive primates existed and lived upon planet earth. From these beings, our very lineage and ascension to becoming the human beings that we are now would have started and it is from these early beings and possibly long before this, that we began our journey.

During the huge time period of around 6–8 million years ago, the first Gorillas came into being, huge primates that once again have aided and assisted in our very arrival and existence into being. It is a testimony to these and several other species that not only have we been conceived and furthered our own journey as humans, but also to the fact that these magnificent beings are still here, living and existing much the same as they would have done since the time of their conception and arrival upon this planet. Chimpanzees would have come into fruition at around this time as well, all adding to the gene pool, as it is factual and well known that humans and several primate species carry over 95% of the same genes, an incredible and undeniable fact that shows us how our survival and mere existence is tantamount to this very majestic, beautiful and very intelligent pool of several slightly different species, all having similar traits and all helping with the arrival of our very own and unique species and race here onto planet earth.

Discoveries have been, are now and always will be being made and it is due to this and new techniques constantly arriving and being invented, that we are now able to almost bring to life previous significances and advancements which lend and help us to understand and arrive at notions and actual evidence of how and why we came into being, along with our evolution into the human beings that we are now. One of these recently unearthed discoveries is several fragments and almost whole bones, including the femoral bone, other fragments of bone and some teeth. These have now been logged, recorded and dated at around 6–8 million years ago and have once again shed light on another species that undoubtedly played a huge part in our own arrival. This species has been called, or categorised as Orrorin Tugenesis. These bones and other evidence show us that this species would have been bipedal, which means able to walk on two legs and stand fairly upright for long periods of time. These new findings have been unearthed, to date, in four different locations, which clearly show that they were fairly widespread and inhabited various locations, which signifies growth, existence and provides us with another link in the chain, bringing us closer still in providing us with very relevant pieces to the jigsaw puzzle that is our very own evolution.

Fossils gathered from a wide array of totally different and vastly widespread archaeological excavation sites, then aged and pieced together where possible, point to the time of 5:5 million years ago and actually bring us to as recently as 14,000 years ago. These pieces strongly indicate and show another part, a strong link and another emergence of the diversity of human evolution. Named 'Proto – Human,' these incredible findings point and show a prehistoric primate, closely resembling humans, although with such a large time period and several closely linked species, it can be difficult to throw much light on these beings as our direct lineage, but with each new discovery, we are able to understand, appreciate and comprehend on a much deeper and intrinsic level, just how we came into being. We cannot deny that all of these varied species had a part to play in the conception and arrival of Mankind onto this planet. If we look at and realise how, with certain species becoming slightly diluted within one of its branches, then it is clear to see that we can see the typical looks, traits and habits of ourselves starting to appear and emerge with what we accept and recognise. Evolution is a huge process and slowly, strain after strain, strong emergence starts to come through, with the weakness at times, of some of the predecessors and originators becoming weaker, being eradicated totally at times sadly. But without all of this manifesting, taking place and coming into being, then we would not be here at all and our very inception would not be one of the greatest stories there is and has been of all time.

With the vastness of the earth and many places still relatively untouched and uninhabited, there are no doubt an infinite number of fossils and other relevant remains that lay deep within the earth's crust, waiting to be found and therefore furthering our understanding of how we came into being and evolved as we have. Science has helped us reach a fairly good comprehension of our journey from millions of years ago, and way back through the aeons of time and has led us to this point now, showing us step by step, how we came to be the way we are now. Obviously some of these vast periods of time, remain a bit vague, although on the whole our conception is very well logged, documented and recognised as a definitive answer to the greatest question there is, this being, where have we come from? Over the years, decades and centuries to come, more and more will be discovered, gifting us a much deeper knowledge and understanding of our arrival to this point in time and how we became human beings.

As recently as 2015, excavations within a cave system in South Africa, have found an incredible amount of skeletal pieces, some of these are almost whole bones, which have aided in the construction and recognition of a now extinct and previously unknown species. Now called 'Homo naledi,' this new species provides us with yet another part of this jigsaw puzzle and will no doubt play a huge part in the piecing together of human evolution across and through the mists of time. This newly found species is characterised by its similar structure, which relates closely to the smaller bodied humans that can be found across the world today. These crucial new findings have been aged at being in existence and living around the approximate time of 2 million years ago and surviving right through to around 900,000 years ago, which is incredible. Once again, this shows that we will always be unearthing new finds that will aid us in our understanding of how we arrived at this point in time, being the way we are. To find out more about this relatively new and truly fascinating species of Hominid beings, check out 'Rising Star Hominids.'

The moulding, shaping and forging of life, within its many guises and appearances, takes time and that is clear to see once we start looking at and researching, where we can and where possible, into the proverbial Pandora's Box, that is the question of how we arrived at this point in time, being in the bodies that we all stand in now. Since time began, our journey has been slowly revealing itself and unravelling through many different and varied shapes, sizes and a wide array of species, most of which have long since died out and are now completely extinct. The only traces are fragments of their long since deceased lives, existence and way of life, fossilised and held within the many layers of Mother Earth. Like the skins of an onion. Slowly we are starting to peel back some of the layers, through findings, research, science and newer discoveries. We will probably never reach the centre and core of this proverbial onion, but to ascertain and slowly unwrap some of the layers, gives us a sense of not only belonging, but also a possible glimpse of our very arrival. As inquisitive beings, it is essential for us to understand, or to try to, and also comprehend where we have come from, how we have been conceived, not just in this life, but through the infinite number of lives that have gone before and paved the way through the mists of time, across the centuries and millennia, slowly showing us our lineage and our ancestry.

The sheer diversity and complexity of how we evolved into the race of Human beings that we are today is nothing short of miraculous and it seems almost incomprehensible really that over millions of years we have slowly arrived at this destination which we find ourselves at now. If we make a comparison to a massive glacier that steadily melts, we can see rivers forming out of the water. These rivers meander, some widen, and some narrow, whereas other ones cease and stop completely. All of the flowing rivers, however large or small, slowly make their way to the sea, the largest body of water that there is. All of these rivers contribute to the seas, even if they cease to be on their journey, as they are merely providing water for the larger and freer flowing rivers to continue their inevitable journey, allowing the natural path and flow of all that is normal to continue and expand when it needs to and as it should.

The huge and vast gene pool that is essential to who and what we are, where we have journeyed from, and where we are at in our evolution now and where we are heading, is incalculable and we are only just starting to scratch the surface on it.

Metamorphosing across the ages and since the very dawn of time, the helical DNA which we will all recognise and which makes us as human beings, would have taken many varied routes and paths, all of these changes that will have arrived at various points in our progress and evolution, have had a massively significant input into creating who and what we are. None of these contributing benefactors,(all of whom are our ancestors), however small, or brief their part was, can be nor should be denied within our journey. However miniscule, whatever period of time they resided and lived in, however long their species may have survived, or however short their span of existence may have been, all of these beings and souls have all played a part in our deliverance, existence and lives which we all have and enjoy today, along with the traits we each have, individual characteristics, feelings, eccentricities and a myriad of other Human complexities. The people we all are today is mainly due to the many beings and diversified species which have all culminated, come together at some point in time and contributed effectively in the making up of not only our story of arrival, but the greater tale of our vast lineage through time.

The 5 Main Stages of Human Evolution

THERE ARE AND have been many, many stages of human evolution. Like single links of an ever increasing length of chain, each one is responsible in crafting, piecing together and forging the ever lengthening chain, slowly forming, as it gets forever longer.

The main stages of our gradual evolution and the key points that clearly define and characterise us as human beings are as follows.

1. Bi-pedalism

One of the most important and extremely significant stages of us becoming so diversified from all other species which we had, and still have, very close links to and are associated with, along with effectively being able to stand alone in our evolution, is just that. From the very first moment we stood upright, the changes were cataclysmic and very symbolic.

Bi-pedalism is the ability to walk and stand unaided and constantly upon two feet. This name comes from the Latin words 'bi,' meaning two, and 'ped' which means foot. When this exactly first came into place is not clear at all, but is thought to be between 4–5 million years ago, although some animal species, birds especially have always been bi-pedal. Other creatures, when needed, have often been able to move fairly freely between four legged, 'quadruped,' and bi-pedal, standing just on their back feet, this was most likely used as a way of accessing higher foliage for food and in defence, if an attack was to take place.

Millions of years ago, once human type beings became signified by standing just on their two feet, many advantages came into place, along with several disadvantages, it is from this that we now became an exclusive species and one of our most definitive traits evolved.

As permanent and habitual bi-peds, apart from newborns who crawl until they have the strength and ability to stand, our bodies have changed and evolved massively. This slow evolution would have been taking place over many years, to allow the first proto type human beings to make the huge cross over and change from occasional standing on two feet, to the transition of having the body strength to undertake it as a permanent fixture and definitive stance.

We can only assume why this huge change took place, but it is widely thought that it happened at about the same time as we started shaping and using tools. This does seem highly likely, as once we stand, we become instantly taller, we can see more, move more easily and our upper bodies then become able to use any tools which may well have been available. Basically we become sleeker and stealthier, all great traits to have and use and in doing this, the whole of our upper bodies can be used for a variety of purposes, holding, carrying, climbing, collecting and being able to see any dangers, simply because our vision instantly becomes wider and not as restricted, as would have been the case while on all fours, effectively crawling.

As well as being able to move much easier, research shows us that walking on two feet, being bi-pedal, takes a lot less energy, in comparison to using four limbs, or feet, a natural progression which helps the body no end. Once we started to stand upright, we would not have had to consume as much food and this explains why we started to move towards other pastimes and activities, all of which have been and were crucial to our existence and survival.

Internally, to allow us to become and remain bi-pedal as a species, very huge and significant changes would have had to take place, another part of our evolution. Our spines would have had to strengthen greatly, simply to allow us to walk permanently upright. The pelvis would have had to gradually reshape, allowing the much freer use of our legs and providing optimum support for us to be able to transport our entire bodies about unaccompanied and at will. The changes that took place over the years were immense and even at the point of standing permanently, there were still a great number of changes to make for us, but smaller adaptations within our own bodies.

2. Losing body hair

Humans are the only hairless primate and in comparison to all other primates, who are totally covered in hair, or fur, this displays another crucial stage in our evolution and yet another defining factor which outlines us and makes us different.

There are several varied and different notions as to why we lost our fur like covering, commonly though, the most accepted reasons are these.

Once we started to elongate our bodies and make the change to standing upright, for several reasons, our diet would have changed. We would have made the transition to eating a more fatty diet. With the introduction of meat, along with being more active in general, our bodies would have naturally built up a fatty layer of skin, which aided in keeping us warm. Over the years after these changes became apparent as part of our daily lifestyles, the fur covering would have lessened greatly. After many, many years, over generations we would have lost the main covering on the larger parts of our bodies almost completely.

Once we lost our furry covering and the layer of body fat came about, insulating us to some extent against the cold weather, our bodies also developed sweat glands; these were needed to make sure that we could effectively cool down. Standing upright made us, as primates, a lot more mobile. Once you take that into consideration, it becomes easier to comprehend further aspects of our own evolutionary process. We would have exercised a lot more, hunting would have kept us moving and once we started to chase and hunt prey, we needed a way to cool down sufficiently and fairly quickly. The endocrine glands are specific sweat glands that help and aid our bodies to cool down by releasing moisture that builds up within our bodies naturally which then evaporate from the skin creating a cooling affect. With exercise heat is built up excessively and without these glands, we would overheat very quickly, our brains would swell which would prove highly dangerous and could ultimately lead to death.

We also, upon being able to stand and walk upon two feet, started to venture further and further out of the relative coolness and shade of the dense forests which our most ancient of ancestors had lived in for many years and still do to this day. Upon widening the areas in which we travelled we would have undoubtedly arrived at some point to the deserts, where there were wide open and uncovered spaces. This could also be and probably is, another major contributor as to why we no longer needed an all over body covering of fur and hair. Had it remained on us, we could not have survived as effectively, once again due to severe over heating of our bodies.

3. Freeing up of our hands

Another vital stage of our evolution belongs to our hands. Once we literally took the first step, or steps, into becoming habitual bi-pedals it freed up the whole of the upper part of our bodies, enabling us to use our hands totally independently and for a multitude of various tasks and different jobs. Over the years, and generations, our hands evolved slowly and much finer movement came into place. Our thumbs elongated in comparison to our primate ancestors who we have ultimately derived from.

The shaping of an assortment of utensils, from the crafting of various tools we would have used, for hunting, drinking and eating, along with a wide range of tasks has helped immensely, aided and gifted us the extremely agile, manoeuvrable and highly dextrous hands that we have ultimately ended up with, all through and because of the gradual process of our own evolution.

4. Crafting and usage of tools

The crafting and shaping of materials, which ultimately brings about the process of making tools is another very subsequent and definitive part of what places us in a unique position compared to other species on the very long and varied path of our evolutionary process. Separately, all of these stages are crucial and imperative to whom we are. Once taken together in their entirety, we can glimpse and understand on a much deeper and intrinsic level, the vast and many varied stages which we have been through. Take nothing away from any of the stages, without a single one of them, the picture of our journey into becoming the humans that we are, could and would not be possible and we would not be standing here today. Some stages really do seem to heighten our understanding of the inception and conception of us as humans. For me personally, this is that stage.

With the introduction of more complex and better crafted tools than had previously been shaped and used, hunting for food became simpler. Mainly due to the reason that the newer tools, spears mainly, would have been sharper and fashioned in a way that would have made launching, or throwing them relatively easy, as the purpose was for killing animals to eat. From this simple, yet very advanced method at the time, new staple foods would have been eaten a lot more frequently and with a reasonable amount of regularity. From this moment, meat, from several various species of animal, would have been caught, killed and enjoyed, providing a much higher intake of protein, which beforehand would have been sporadic and lacking in consistency. Diets now would radically change from this moment onwards.

Hunting also brings about a greater need, or it would have at this time, of social interaction. Working together, often closely, to chase down, trap and kill the animals which were prevalent at that time. If we look at these fairly slight changes within our evolution, then combine them with the other critical stages of our evolutionary path, we can envisage and understand, how our brains would have needed to grow and evolve as well, which obviously shows us further that our skulls, which were relatively different beforehand, had to reshape and restructure to house and encompass our now rapidly enlarged brains.

Once social interaction had started properly, it would have carried on and evolved fairly quickly, diverging from primitive grunts, spreading out into a more appreciated and recognised language and hand gestures, which would have been evolving constantly. With all the other changes as well, our brains were rapidly growing, This could, and probably was, the point at which the human species developed what we now term as the brains frontal cortex. It is this which designates and makes us stand alone from all other species and allows us to have the level of higher thinking, analysis, empathy and many other vital traits, which the majority of other species are lacking in.

5.   Dilution and sexual selection

The very gene pool which we have slowly and steadily arrived from and out of is vast, infinite almost and the many diversified and varied species which we were and are still fairly closely linked to, and still to this day carry certain traits from, is massive. Millions of years of evolution has made sure that we, Human beings, as a species, stand here today as a reminder and in memory of many extinct genus and breeds that unknowingly participated and played a part, however small, in moulding and shaping who and what we are today, therefore gifting and allowing us to survive, to form, grow and evolve in the many complex ways in which we have. Like an enormous jigsaw puzzle, if we didn't now carry all those pieces, we would not and could not be as we are now. Quite simply the picture of us as the human species, and our long and complex evolutionary journey, would not be complete and whole.

The dilution of where we have come from to where we are today as a species would have been a very slow and gradual process, that much is clear and obvious. We only have to look at the shaping and appearance of our ancestors (through remains, skeletons and other findings, reliable pictures and historic relevance has been gathered, put together and catalogued to record our arrival and the slow dilution, eradication with some species linked to us) to see how over the years, the main characteristics of our own human group, or collection that has emerged, strengthened and remained as we know it and is now a recognisable and dominant force within nature and creation as a whole.

For any genus to arrive as a collective, stay that way and remain totally recognisable as we know it, sexual selection is required and this takes a long time. Generation after generation would have had to choose, or select another member of the same species to effectively breed, or mate with. Nowadays, we take this for granted without even thinking about it, simply because there are no other choices, so we don't need to consider, or plan it. Once we look at pictures and images, constructed through skeletons found over time, some dating back several million years , it becomes clear to see how our lineage has radically changed and morphed from the earliest almost Human forms, through the ages to where we have arrived at now. We can then start to appreciate and see many of the traits and features which millions of years ago were very prominent in facial structure, composition and skeletal resemblance to our selves. Then with careful selection and inter breeding, the dilution, or watering down slowly of various other groups within our own collective, becomes less and less as each new generation breeds within its own genus, leading to us now, which as a race is now totally recognisable and plain to see.

This extremely slow process came about basically from several different aspects. The main ones are these key points and five definitive stages which combined and amalgamated together, show us just how we slowly started becoming and evolving into the Human form which we all recognise, appreciate and are today. The culmination of bi-pedalism, losing our bodily hair covering, using our hands for finer movements, the forming of our brains, restructuring of our skulls and skeletal structure, the strengthening of the earliest communications that were used, all of these traits which combined together, helped us emerge as humans. Then the slow introduction of inter breeding, or sexual selection, made sure that we shed the other characteristics, features and traits which our ancient primitive Ancestors carried and were clearly visible within our closely linked groups until fairly recently on the time scale of our emergence as a race.

Upon reflection, it is clear to see how we came about, shaped the forms we are in now that we recognise so easily and readily, but we must not over look what an incredible journey that each one of our Ancestors, however ancient or primitive they may seem, went through. Many parts were played and with our deliverance to now, many species have become extinct as we slowly chose to select our sexual partners, effectively breeding out the characteristics that were no longer needed, wanted or desired for our Human group to become strong and ensure our survival as we now know it. This dilution was a necessity, imperative and had to happen, yet we must not take anything away from the various species which participated, however briefly (and many now no longer in existence), in our slow emergence and arrival into our Human forms. All of these species, however recent or ancient, are all of our Ancestors and without one single strand of each one, then we would not be here now in the guise that we stand in today.

Biology of Human Evolution – Characteristics and Genetics

The human form is an easily recognisable, yet extremely varied breed, the human gene pool, if we look back through time to our conception and beyond, is vast and an almost incomprehensible subject and topic. From the very dawn of time a seemingly infinite number of species, of many varied types have had a part to play, not only in our arrival, but the starting and very emergence of the traits, shaping, moulding, features and easily recognisable attributes which our Human group, or collective, carries now that we are all instilled and equipped with. Paleoanthropology is the study of our culture as Humans, how our species as a whole is made up. The characteristics, such as our common traits which we can be deemed by and distinguished from, also our core and base behaviours, all of these predominant and main features are crucial and vital to us as a breed, species, or genus, as they are to all groups of life. Without all, or any of these traits, we would be unrecognisable and would not be the force within nature and the universe which we are now and have been for many, many generations.

BIOLOGY

The biology of us as a group, as with any species, is the understanding of not only who and what we are, but the grouping, knowledge and discovery of traits which provides us with a much more specific understanding, and realisation, of where we have emerged and what we are derived from.

Looking back upon the possibly infinite species and sub species which have all had a part to play in our creation and manifestation into the group of human beings that we are now is a vast topic to cover and would be hotly debated, as it has been in the past and for many years now. So to make it relatively easier to understand, I will just strip back all of the countless strands of species, far too numerous to mention, and take it back to basics, which is ultimately our common Ancestor. Evolution and biology show us that all the various and vast multitudes of life forms emerge and spring from one common Ancestor, this analogy and comprehension is often termed and referred to as 'The Tree of Life,' the base from which we and all other genus groups and species have derived from – biogenesis.

Gorilla's and chimpanzees are our closest relatives, that much is well known and documented. From this point though, we can grasp that slowly and steadily, that branch of our Tree of Life started to grow with the introduction of other Hominid species, a lot of whom are now extinct. Yet we can see that with interaction and cross breeding, the known Human form slowly and surely started to come about and evolve. As recently, or as far back as discoveries show us, 5–6 million years ago hominid groups were starting to walk on two legs, stand on two feet and were beginning the slow ascension into the forms we know now, showing the relatively primitive yet base behaviours which we can clearly accept and recognise as early close cousins and ancestors of our own lineage.

This very topic, subject and study of biology provides us with a platform from which we can see how we and other species came into being, how we evolved and how we reached and gathered all the now common attributes, physically and mentally, along with key features and traits which we can all recognise and are comfortable with. It is relatively easy for us now to comprehend all of this as we can see where we have come from. For the great minds that first discovered our inception, conception and metamorphosis though, they had to slowly and painstakingly observe and study archaeological findings along with ancient remains and slowly track back to find all of this out. An arduous yet very rewarding journey which has taken centuries to piece together to ultimately discover the vast path which began millions of years ago and has only fairly recently come to fruition with our emergence as the human species as a whole. It is from all this tracing back our lineage to the first and original branch of our Ancestry, that makes it straight forward for us to start at that point way back in the aeons of time, that a simplified and conceptual, recognisable understanding and appreciation of where and how we emerged has been gifted to us. It is a far less difficult task to look forward from those several million years ago when we can clearly see our emergence within and from the Tree of Life, to what it would have been and is to trace it back, piece by piece as many people have done over the years. Yet without their hard work, persistence, patience and discovery, we would not now have and be able to refer as easily to where we have come from, which shows us just how we came into being. It is this very study and intricate understanding that has delivered us our own Human Biology as a reference and case study.

The greatest story or tale that has ever been told is, along with the many aspects and alternatives of our humble arrival and beginnings, the fascinating and infinite subject of just how we as a species emerged into life, first drew breath and slowly started gathering momentum as we travelled through the times which saw us branch off and away from our primitive and ape like cousins.

Once we shift into a totally different and plausible mindset, where we can view and digest parts of our own journey and inception, then the whole wondrous story of not only who we are as a species now, but the incredible and miraculous journey through the shrouds of time becomes alive with recognition. The transformations we have succumbed to and been through as a whole genus lineage is so humbling and mind boggling. Yet when we look upon this journey we have embarked upon through time, we can understand and start to realise that our discoveries into just who and what we are, are only just beginning. Basically, the discoveries found, the science that we know now and use to carbon date, place and record events and log, are only really scratching the surface and our findings are only just starting.

As we age and time moves on, more and more findings, skeletal remains and such like will inevitably be unearthed and come to light, then slowly, as our sciences move on, along with our understandings, as they do, the whole story of our emergence, piece by piece, will start to slowly form and an immense, almost infinite jigsaw puzzle will be gradually built up, forming a huge tapestry, where strand by strand, thread by thread, our story as a species will be built up and laid out for us all to see, acknowledge, respect and honour.

The biology and intricate weavings of our very emergence is slowly before our eyes being discovered already, shared and explained to us. It is these absolutely amazing findings, workings, datings and knowledge which we now have access to, that can truly divulge, open up to us all as a whole species and show us just how we came into being, along with how we split off from the original Tree of Life branch which we stem from and cast light upon how we took the decision to build, create and morph into one of the most complex species and wondrous lineage of beings which we all know and are today.

Without the science of biology, along with the great minds that have and still are discovering and recording just where it is we have ultimately come from, our own curious thoughts and mindset that set us on a journey of discovery, along with our own yearning as individuals to understand, absorb and perceive just where and how it is we came into being, we simply would not have a clue and would remain in a stasis of nonchalance and almost ignorance of who and what we are.

It is this biology, coupled with our own base inquisitiveness, that has since time began, led us through dangerous times, shown us the way, strengthened our spirits and guile, enhanced our characteristics and made us become the incredible genus and collective species which we are today.

Just look and reflect upon our inception into the world, our original branch of the Tree of Life which we stemmed from and have emerged. We have fused together with countless other pieces and parts of that same Tree, we have then, as a Tree, or solitary branch does, shed and cast off some various layers of bark, then we have grown and reformed once again, changing shape, mutating, elongating and growing constantly, allowing us to make advancements along the way and gifting us the ability, both physically and metaphysically, to reshape and mould ultimately into the incredible genus which we are today.

Cast your mind's eye into what is basically our gene pool, imagine that you can view the incalculable array of different species which we have derived and ultimately emerged from, an immense and stupendous collection of what are now our ancestors, however small their part was, yet we must not take anything away from each strand, or droplet from the gene pool which we have amalgamated and stemmed from. All of these beings helped and assisted with our forming, without a single one of them, we would not be, it's impossible, not as we are now anyway and it is the miraculous science and studying of biology that is slowly piecing together, recording and showing us just how vast the pool of where we have come from is and as time slowly goes by and carries on, more and more threads will be revealed and the understanding we have of our own lineage, will deepen and strengthen with this accordingly as time, coupled with the advancements of science, shows us what is the greatest story ever told and proclaims to us the many Ancestors we have as a group and collective species.

CHARACTERISTICS

The characteristics we all have, carry and display are what make us individuals. Obviously as a species we have a certain build, make up and basic structure that ensures we are identifiable as a race. Within that though, we all have traits, idiosyncrasies, eccentricities and individualised ways. Across the spectrum, these base traits can be seen and viewed through many people and Humans as a whole. It is these small differences, perceptions and envisagings of the world, what we have been through and witnessed that rubber stamp our inputs and outputs into the world and make us stand alone and solitary in comparison to all others.

Again we are looking at such a diversified array of characteristics and in a sense, a lot of these faculties and quirks which we display are what can be deemed to compartmentalise us and bring about our very own lineage of Ancestry. The colour of hair we have, our eye colour, bone structure, height, build, weight, all of these and a huge amount of other peculiarities too numerous to mention, ensure that we as individuals can look back, reflect upon and nowadays with the countless and easily accessed records we can look into, can define us as solitary beings as having threads and strands of our very own lineage and personalised Ancestry, which is incredible and helps to show us not only how our race came into being, but how our very own branch of the Tree of Life has formed, grown and evolved down through the ages. This gifts us an insight into those individuals who have now passed on, but played a huge part in our own life force, along with the very shaping and delivering of us to just who and what we are now.

As there is with any particular genre, subject, or topic, there is almost a blueprint, an idealised archetypal image which sets the basic pattern of that given subject. Within Humanity, in its many forms and guises, there is an archetypal figure head that anybody can easily recognise and adhere to and it has been that way through the ages. Like an outline which encompasses all of our regularities, a body, arms, legs, hands, a mouth, eyes, nose, ears, etc, this we all know and even though the base and core patterning of our skeletal and molecular build up remains steadfast and carved in stone, so to speak, it is the other, often miniscule, if visible to the naked eye, vast array of differences throughout each person and individual varieties of colour, shaping, size, muscle formation, stance and visible appearances that let us stand out from the crowd and within our own skin. Before we even hear and listen to that person speak, or spend time in their company, it is these unique and personalised characteristics that distinguish each and every one of us and configure us as solitary beings and individual humans within our own right, simply because of these characteristics.

These individual quirks and attributes we all have within and without our physical selves, have been slowly forming through the scale of time and here I am referring to what we have on the outside of our bodies, our visible characteristics. Our very structure, barring any ailments that might make us stand differently, or may make us seem disfigured in the eyes of some people, has been forming and shaping through the aeons of time and it is these features which are all part of and form the branches of our very own ancestry, our heritage and our own lineage.

At some point within our own personal life's journey, I have no doubt we would have heard a parent or family member say that we, or another person has got certain shaping of maybe an ear, mouth, smile, etc, of a well known and regarded member of a particular side of the family, incorporated with looks and similarities that can be put down and referred to as part of the other string, or side of the lineage line from which we have risen from and are descended from, which clearly shows us that the forming and shaping of our own bodily forms, can be linked and closely related to and shows where our direct ancestry lays.

This is undoubtedly another highly infinite and truly fascinating part of not only who we are as individuals, but now we can start to proverbially strip down, pull back and start to explore the immense journey which has played out even before we have arrived and breathed our first breath within this mortal body and upon this earthly coil and realm.

Once we have reached an understanding, along with recognition of this humbling journey that was playing out long before our arrival here, we can and do often start to make comparisons.

Basically we can look at photographs of our families, just with a different aspect and view of it all. We start to see common ground, familiar looking features within our families, those that are still living and are around us, also we can often sense in a different light and way almost, particular physical traits and well formed bodily characteristics from our family members who sadly now are passed away, deceased and are no longer with and around us in a physical bodily form.

Once we have this close connection and a much deeper resonance and intrinsic, almost heightened awareness of not only who we are, but where we have journeyed from way back in the mists of time to now, we can and undoubtedly do start to reflect deeper. Then the realisation of our hereditary and direct lineage comes into play and it is entirely up to us then, as individuals, to journey back and explore our own ancestry to which ever degree we wish to, or if we combine both sets of parents, an amazing journey then awaits to unfold and unravel right before our eyes.

The characteristics we have and which distinguish and personalise who we are and where we have emerged from, symbolise not only ourselves, but each person who has played a part in our conception and aided, or gifted us with these traits, markings and features which stand out and basically highlight who we are and who has aided our journey of deliverance to now.

Physical attributes, shapings and features deem us with uniqueness and totally personalise who we are and if it was possible, we could see and envisage how our lineage and different branches of our ancestry have gained their physical characteristics way back since the dawning of mankind. Some personal features would have radically changed over time, that's inevitable, mainly through different chains and lines of breeding weakening some quirks, while strengthening other physical traits.

If the line has stayed relatively strong and not been too tampered with over recent generations, we could clearly see family chains evolving, forming and coming to fruition, therefore giving us distinguishable characteristics which can be easily viewed within photographs of family members and relatives, both living and deceased.

If we move away now from the physical and easily seen characteristics which our bodies clearly hold and readily display, we can then start to look at and maybe grasp an understanding of the many other traits, singular and individual characteristics which all contribute to make up just who and what we are, from this we can also run parallels to our Ancestors and our own lineage.

As spiritual beings, which we are first and foremost, it is essential and vital to show our inner selves, especially when you consider the fact that around 93% of communication is non verbal. Admittedly a large proportion of what we hold inside our souls, inner beings and our minds is learnt and processed from this lifetime, yet many of our inner, deep and often hidden characteristics will have been passed down through and from our direct lineage, which gifts us with a basic blueprint. A lot of this goes way back, an example is our primeval need and desire to survive, often in the face of adversity. Another very primitive example is us, as a species loving and being drawn to fire, this has to transcend anything we have learnt here in this body and can only be traced back to the dawning of humanity and our very primitive and base core of keeping warm and staying safe.

For many of us who have taken the incredible journey of tracing our family trees, we can and invariably do discover some amazing similarities, often not just with comparisons to ourselves, but also the intricately weaved threads which bind a lot of lineages together. These traits can and often do show and reveal themselves through not just one generation, but can be pinpointed and found in several. Often these peculiarities and depths of character cross over and can be seen mirrored in the parallel of the other side of our lineage and ancestry as well. Common features, all of which gives us a shared focal point and from these discoveries we can make the assumptions that it is a build up of this biological data that is now displayed within ourselves, endorsing the very fact that we are mainly made up of and created by and because of others, truly fascinating.

We can often find ourselves favouring a particular colour, longing to fulfil ourselves with a strong yearning for a specific job, or career. We can also feel the pull to live somewhere we may never have been. All these longings, yearnings and questions stem from somewhere and it is plausible and totally acceptable that often, when we trace our history and open up the proverbial Pandora's Box that is our ancestry and lineage, that we can see and discover that many of those feelings and senses we harbour and hold, have been imbued from those who have gone before, yet their legacy remains within us.

From the many traits that we possess deep within our psyche, feelings, mannerisms, maybe short tempers, loud resonating voices, love of different genres, smells, places and a whole host of other unseen and misunderstood idiosyncrasies, we can, if we look and trace back, often find likenesses to our ancestors. If we decide to reconnect with our pasts and gift life into these beings, our families, we can learn so much from them and in doing this, we can invariably learn so much more about who and what we are. Not just where we have come from, but greater lessons of why we are the way we are and often, why we act the way in which we do.

Our fundamental beings hold and contain a plethora of other beings. We know that, sadly, many of those will be overlooked, forgotten and will remain undiscovered, in this lifetime anyway. If we begin though to scratch the surface and set out on the journey to discover who made and shaped us into the beings which we all are today, we connect and resonate much more deeply within ourselves, our ancestors and the universe as a whole. If we do ultimately decide to do this, we are turning over long hidden stones that have almost been forgotten in the mists of time, yet once we turn these stones of discovery over, we can start to clearly see how our path was formed and forged way back in time. This path that we ultimately find ourselves upon and walking now, was crafted and gifted to us over countless generations and effectively it lays before us now, although in the past, for us to step upon and discover how the proverbial stone that began our journey was laid and how we have, unbeknown to us before, had our lives mapped out for us, along with all of the individual characteristics we have, whether that is in our physical appearance, or the often hidden inner and deeper depths which we all possess.

GENETICS

We all carry and, are formed accordingly, by what is now commonly termed and known as 'The Double Helix' or DNA. It is these base formations that grow accordingly and then determine what group of species, sub species, or type of matter we are to belong to, grow and evolve as, and which predetermine just who and what we are in the physical and molecular form.

These two strands, or the combination together which is the double helix, contain alternating groups of sugars, phosphates and nitrogen basically and it is these that are the key to all life, structure and formation. Within these tightly linked, cavorting together, yet separate strands, or the very base threads that weave all life formed, they hold our predetermined lineage and heredity, which is the passing on of all the traits, mental and physical which we all ultimately possess that have been gifted to us from the generations before, parents, grand parents and so on, our ancestors combined, culminated together and then the baton of life and existence is passed on to us to carry on that line.

Genetics is the study of the DNA structure and formation which we all have and carry, as does all life and living forms. It is the understanding of biological molecules and how they form and are passed on from one generation to another and how they determine the constant evolution of us and all life, which again brings us to heredity and lineage. The traits and oddities which we all encompass, hold within and display are formed into are ultimately from the DNA molecules within us, which includes the genes we all carry and are part of us.

Once we group together these understandings and sciences, it does become much clearer and easier to comprehend, how we are formed, why we have been formed and born as we were. This also helps us to grasp the reasons we carry so many individualised and personalised characteristics, which are more often than not, passed onto and down to us from our lineage and our direct branch, or branches of our own ancestry.

Creation and Origin Myths

THE WEB OF life and all that has gone before is indeed a very rich tapestry that contains an infinite number of threads and yarns, woven, embroidered and stitched together. Each one of these metaphysical threads is representational to all beings that have gone before, the many cataclysmic events that have manifested and played out since the beginning of time. Yet within this very rich and invisible tapestry, there is an immeasurable number of myths which relate to and are extremely varied in just how the world first came into being along with our own conception, birthing and placing as a species into this life and upon this beautiful earth and planet.

The inestimable number of origin myths that spread over and around the world, contained within all societies and cultures, is incredible. Over time, many of these myths would have changed, as the very word 'myth' tends to portray a subject, or topic that originally manifested orally and was told to the specific group that first originated it. Over time, these often fireside tales were passed on through each generation and ultimately the subtleties change, become embellished and enriched. The base core would have remained steadfast though, with no real deviations from that, it is just the peripherals that alter. Then the myths become elongated and enhanced, more often than not, this is done to keep up with the changing times, society and world around us, simply to enhance the tales and as with any genre, or specified subject, slight interpretations tend to creep in, as you would expect them to simply because orating is only defined by the tale teller and will invariably change each and every time it is told to an audience.

As time passed, the scribed and written word started to creep in, across many cultures and society as a whole. It is at this point, and I find it very sad indeed, that the power of the written word started to become recognised. This has ultimately had a double edge to it, as most things do. The incredible tales and stories of mythology that were endorsed within many diversified cultures could now be written down and recorded for posterity and kept alive over time as a way of enriching lives and pinpointing a tribe's, or village's origin myth, that would have had their very own take and interpretation of it. On the negative side of this, the written word encouraged some groups within society to implement lavish stories which only serve to control and muster power over people, basically indoctrinating them. If they don't conform to these idealistic and often radicalised ideas, writings and enforcements, they are judged, shunned, ignored and at times worse, persecuted, tortured and killed, simply because they won't conform to another's way of thinking.

I find it very comforting, that so many of these myths have been saved and are now available in the written context and they are still accessible to all. It is also heart warming that even though we now live in an extremely rich and decadent world, many cultures and the sub cultures that live alongside one another, have their own takes and slight abbreviations within what is often the same tale or myth. Yet there are no opposites, just pure and unadulterated coexistence and each group, or side is content in the knowledge that origin myths are still being kept alive, providing a backbone to their specific culture, which reflects their ancestors beliefs and ideas and also can endorse and placate strength to who they are and also how they live their lives to this day.

One of the most sought after answers that humanity and human kind have been trying to answer and establish since time began, is how our Universe that along with the multiple planets, stars and other galaxies first came into being, and then how did we first arrive, multiply, forge and evolve?

As you would expect with any such question, there are multiple, diverse and very different answers, hypotheses and theories, none of which are wrong to those individuals that believe and practice them, however obscure they may seem for many. If that belief, faith, or tradition resonates within them, then that is just fine and portrays further what an amazing and very varied planet that we all inhabit and are blessed to live upon.

The Christian belief, along with its many interpretations and guises, as well as the Jewish and Islamic faiths, all hold a firm belief that there was one creator, God, and over a six day period, he shaped, moulded and created the world, the Universe and all the trees, rivers, mountains, animals, insects, all life as we know it, including us as human beings. Then on the seventh day, he took a rest and marvelled at what he had achieved. To highlight an interpretation of this belief (which there is usually within the multiple faiths we have in and across our world today), another take on this is that God created a solitary man who was called Adam. God made Adam out of earth, he then took one of Adams ribs and made Eve, who was to be Adam's equal, only in a feminine form and body. However we personally view and perceive this tale, or myth, we cannot dispute that this is one of the most widely appreciated and well known origin myths throughout the world as we know it. Millions and millions of people around the globe follow this tale and the book which contains the teachings that accompany the various stories from the beginning when this God created the world and all life contained within it. Commonly known as The Bible, this book forms the basis and the backbone for the Christian belief system and structure, along with the slightly different variations and interpretations which there are. These can be found and viewed in different formats and all versions are highly regarded and closely followed, believed and practiced by the majority of people around the globe to this day.

In Aboriginal creation and mythology tales, which again there are slight variations of, even though, these similar tales entwine, run parallel and harmonise with each other, we can hear how closely this group of people, along with their whole culture, live within the natural world, harnessing and incorporating, (basically honouring and working with, not against,) the riches and elements of the natural world around them. Constantly giving thanks for their long lineage, all that they have and are, while knowing just where they have journeyed from, thanks to their ancestors, who they call upon and show honour to constantly.

According to findings which have been unearthed and ancient cave paintings, along with relatively primitive etchings, it is widely believed and regarded that humans first reached Australia for the first time around 50,000 years ago.

It is said that these people were nomadic and stemmed from a long line of heredity, which can be linked back to the original tribe, or culture which had inhabited Australia for many centuries before hand. They spoke many languages and had, over time, devised a relatively complex society, yet a society which remained within the circumferences of the natural world and all that lived and dwelled within it, again constantly giving thanks for everything that they were, had and all the beauty that lies within and around the natural world. Alongside this culture, the aboriginals developed a nature based and natural religion, which is still followed by their people today. Anthropologists have deemed this religion as the longest enduring throughout history, one which is still followed and practiced to this day and is highly regarded as their way of life.

The Aboriginal creation and origin myth harkens back to a time when the world was just a huge lump of mud, along with clay, a world totally devoid of life, colour and darkness, in a word, there was nothing. This time is referred to and known to all Aboriginal tribes as the 'Dreamtime,' a time before existence, way before the world was shaped, formed and created.

Within and from this cocoon like stasis, aboriginal ancestors, or spirits rose up and slowly formed the richly imbued landscapes that we have in the world today, slowly shaping the rivers, hills, forests. Sculpting what was a harsh and devoid world, turning it into a very beautiful place, full of colour, rich with elemental force. Then, once they had created the world, they then gifted and gave life to all creatures and Humanity.

This incredible group and race of people that we know as Aboriginal, still closely follow and honour the lessons which have been instilled within them, they only take from the bountiful Earth what they need to ensure survival, while constantly giving thanks and honouring all creation. These people believe that they are all descended from the original ancestors and spirits which shaped and forged the natural world, gifting us all with life, languages and all that there is. A culture which does and always has had extremely close links to their own lineage, where the tales still not only survive, but are readily shared and told to each new generation. This humble group, tribe, or society believe that to coexist and know the world and all the wonder contained within it, that you have to trace back your ancestry, find and establish your roots. For it is knowing where you have come from that will ultimately endow you with the strength, clarity and knowledge to know where you are heading. This very practice and belief, is termed as the 'Song line,' it is this knowledge and way of being for them, which encompasses all life and shows the journey taken by their ancestors, along with being the backbone and base core structure of their creation and origin myth.

Within Greek mythology, the creation tale takes on a widely diverse series of events, depending once again on where we source our information from and even this can often only add to the confusion and chaos, which is more or less the only tangible outcome that we can arrive at, that before creation, the Greeks believe that there was only a state of chaos within the Universe.

This creation and myth of the worlds conception, which ancient Greeks believed vehemently, brings into play the infinite number of gods, goddesses and multiple deities which we all know. The early Greeks strived to live their lives within their teachings, often attempting to personify these mythological beings within their own physicality, along with living their daily lives according to which god, or goddess was more prevalent at that time, believing that they would then be imbued and empowered directly with the many traits these deities were seen to harness and possess.

One of the most widely viewed interpretations of the inception of creation from Greek mythology, is that Gaia, (who many of us will know from our own faiths and traditions is Mother Earth) and Uranus (the sky) combined forces from out of the darkness and state of chaos that the Universe was held in before the light came, and had between them, many offspring, children, all of which were twins.

The chaos upon this creation myth only seems to accelerate upon the actual creation of the world and Universe. Unfortunately, some of the children had a strong dislike of their siblings and their apparent father. This stemmed into cruelty, anger and resulted in maiming, along with apparent deaths caused by pure jealousy and hatred. Then from these brutal confrontations, other aspects and parts of the Universe were created and came into being.

Greek mythology is truly alive and riddled with an infinite number of deities, many of which are still well known to this day, across the world. Within this though, there are many multiples of gods and various goddesses who play vital parts and are still revered, or honoured to this day. Which shows us again, however obscure or unfeasible a lot of these myths and tales may seem of our conception and very creation, or appear to us now, they have all stood the test of time and are widely known, called upon and worshipped, no matter what our own and personal take on them is.

One of the most harmonious, heart warming and believable creation and origin myths there is, has to be the Buddhist faiths tale of non-arrival, a state of simply being. The Buddhist tradition doesn't have one as such, merely an abundance of spiritual and higher consciousness teachings that are readily available to us all, through easily accessed, yet highly practiced, followed, absorbed and honoured insights. All of which are inside each one of us and are there for us all to discover. If we can reach and achieve a grasp of spiritual enlightenment within this body vessel, then we can attune ourselves to the higher self, which their belief and faith shows us is the key to ourselves and a far richer, deeper and more intrinsic link to the very source of all being and life, that being the Universe, along with all the multitude of beauty, questions and answers which all lay there, which we can all tap into if we choose to.

The Buddhist belief is nature based and from this, we can see how their daily lives, teachings and aspirations manifest outwardly and are encompassed within who they are. Following closely, and adhering to, the vibration and uncomplicated ways of the natural world, which we are all a part of and can easily access in an instant.

If there was an actual creation and origin myth for these highly spiritually developed and accomplished beings, then that would ultimately be derived from the world and Universe around them, simplistic, achievable, believable and very orthodox. It would be, and is, nature based. There lies the answers and key to all that we strive to be and become, basically at one with the world, with ourselves, others and all life as we know and understand it.

One of the main features of the Buddhist belief, which, if we were to consider as a form of origin and creation, is that there is no beginning and no end, therefore everything has always been in place and we have always existed, be it in one form or another and in various guises, everything just has been, is now and will carry on. Within that very belief though, we are shown and taught, within ourselves and by the Universe, that we should comprehend the greater meanings of life, the wider world and all the humble creations contained and living within that very concept.

Based and structured around the natural world, this belief is widely regarded and highly respected around the globe and has been for centuries. Providing comfort, wisdom and a way to allow the self to become free from the shackles and ties of other indoctrinations. It offers wisdom and insights to many, without the need to conform, just a realisation that resonates deep within our own psyche, our hearts, minds and higher spiritual selves.

To attune yourself with the hypothesis, culture and belief that there was no creation and origin is remarkable, within all of the aspects and ideologies. There is a base core belief that we begin afresh, as the world does, with each new dawning and, furthermore, with each and every action that we undertake and act out into our surroundings and Universe as a whole. A kind of kinetic energy theory really, simplified yet highly diverse in all of its attributes.

For every action, there is a reaction and once we can fully comprehend this fact along with only being, living and showing positivity, then the world would be a much better place to live in. This belief begs the question and answers it fully within its simplicity. We were not created; there is no beginning and no end. It is what we do in-between that truly matters. Live within the parameters of the natural world, taking onboard and encompassing the lessons we have gifted to us, then we can learn, grow and evolve, through this life and in all our lives to come.

The Celtic tradition is widely followed and practiced throughout several cultures and societies within the modern world to this day, as it has been for many, many centuries. To actually find and determine a Celtic creation or origin myth is extremely difficult. However there are, apparently, a few very brief tales, whether or not they actually stem from the original polytheism (more than one god) Celtic tradition and way of life, is not very well known. Unfortunately, due to the Roman invasions across mainland Europe around two millennia ago, the origins of Celtic belief and way of life have been more or less eradicated as many Celts were put to the sword by the Romans. It is almost impossible to tell now whether or not the many deities, gods and goddesses which form the vast threads of Roman beliefs, were actually taken from the Celtic system of worship, which many of them do bare striking similarities to and there are a countless number of them. This is something we can never fully be sure of, yet thanks to a revival from neo-pagans around the world, new books written are now containing research and various explanations which seem highly plausible and carry strong resemblances to several deities that could well have formed the backbone and infrastructure to the Celtic belief system.

One fairly loose Celtic creation myth that might have survived, although this is subject once again to beliefs and various interpretations, is that before the arrival of mankind and all life, there was the Earth and there were the oceans. At a point, where the sea met the land, the waves crashed onto and upon the shore, this resulted in the sea spray foaming vigorously and intensely, so much so that a pure white mare was born from the sea foam, her name was Eiocha.

Cernunnos is known widely as 'The Horned God,' he is also representational of the stag, masculine virility and strength, along with being the male based deity believed in a lot of Celtic tales to be the God, or Lord of the forests, trees and vegetation.

A union between Eiocha and Cernunnos occurred and from this, other deities emerged in various shapes, sizes and guises, all representational of elements and aspects we all know and are aware of within creation and the natural world around us. Unfortunately though, it is at this point where stories and any specific Celtic creation and origin myths become very vague, is this because of the Roman invasion and apparent massacres which ensued. We will never know.

As with most beliefs, faiths and traditions, however obscure, distant and vague they may seem, they are all still closely followed and respected by countless numbers of people today and have been for many centuries before. These myths are now receiving resurgence within today's very modernistic societies, simply because we are all different, which shows that obviously we all need and want to have something different to follow and worship, rather than the often non resonation that the main stay religions have to offer. There is nothing right, nor wrong about another's beliefs, so long as they are not used for control, extortion and wrong doing. With so many beliefs though, it is very clear and apparent, that many over-lay others, which brings about lines which are often blurred. This can then prove almost impossible to determine which paths are the most likely to have their origins within those parameters. This is where coexistence has to be accepted and honoured, which makes it daunting, almost unachievable to allocate these distinctive, yet also similar faiths as having totally viable and separate creation and origin myths. Quite simply, if something draws you towards it and resonates deep within your very essence, accept and follow it, regardless of whether or not there is a pre-determined and pinpointed area of origin.

Regardless of which faith we hold dear to us and may follow, we cannot ignore the wonderful array of creation myths and tales that are woven throughout the world and widely interspersed areas and regions of society, along with differing cultures, tribes and the various pockets of human inhabited lands across the world. Each one of these tales, irrespective of our own personal belief system, truly show what an incredible world in which we live. For these tales to have been birthed in the first place is totally humbling, let alone the fact that many of them are revered today. Maybe even more so now, as they provide strength, along with a vital support to billions of people worldwide, who maybe otherwise could find themselves struggling with the ever changing and expanding ways of society. These myths and wondrous tales of creation and our very core origins hold ideas and premonitions of plausible concepts, which allow the individuals to believe, or not how humanity and mankind as a species came into being. So long as we adhere to the crux of these numerous creation origins and beliefs that we follow, along with allowing ourselves to walk our own paths with honour, integrity and a peaceful heart, then we are giving respect totally to the very ancestors who crafted all of these myths and granted us our own lives and lineage to explore and retrace.

Ancestors of Tomorrow

THE CONTRASTING VARIANTS which can reveal a lot of our ancestry to us, as a whole group of beings and also our individual lineage with which our own ancestors by direct bloodline can be discovered, is an amazing quest and remarkable challenge to unfold if we choose to undertake it. I find it astounding that one day soon, we will all be a part of that same group and mass of now passed away beings that will become termed as 'ancestors.'

The infinite legions which stand in accordance and as an everlasting tribute to the lives we now have and live each day, show us that our very survival is tantamount to holding the nucleus of mankind as a species. If we consider each individual life as a singular thread contained within the vast and extremely decadent tapestry that displays our emergence into being millions of years ago, we can see just how vital every single strand is and has been. Remove one solitary stitch and the whole image crumbles. It is not complete, therefore the whole picture fails. To diversify; the crux of our whole being, past, present and future is only possible with everyone playing their part, however miniscule and insignificant they may seem. Or, at times, we can view ourselves that way, as not mattering. This simply is not the case and we are all paramount to what happens within the world, society, our lineage and our ancestry as a whole.

It is we who are alive today that hold the key to our existence in the future and for the generations that are to come. We are the ancestors of tomorrow.

We are now living in what can only be viewed as the very best of times (within that there is a flip side, just to level out the balance that is contained within all life and creation). Our world is full of incredible technology with which we can talk to anybody anywhere at any time. The discoveries that are being made and found constantly allow us to further our education and we are now free to explore anywhere we wish, or want to, both physically and metaphysically. Never before has there been so much information available and so easily sourced and fully accessible to all.

Within all of this, we can now truly appreciate what those who have gone before gave and instilled deep within us as a race of beings. The extremely rich and once invisible tapestry that has been embroidered since our very conception into and upon this beautiful planet is now so clear to see, that it is almost visible to the naked eye.

From what can only be described as an extremely slow, yet steady, almost cacophonic start, our ancestors slowly emerged, survived against all odds at times, yet remained staunch and steadfast, resilient to their surroundings and all that nature and the world placed in their way. They had to fight, win and lose, yet still our predecessors rose up and found the inner gall to carry on. These ancient beings that form our ancestry as a collective ensured we would emerge at some time, as we have and in effect, they laid the stepping stones for all of humanity as a species. Without any one of them, we would and could not be, each one of them has ethereally handed us the baton of creativity by gifting us our mere existence and life which we all have today.

We are now the guardians and keepers of all the knowledge that was held by the ancestors, all the life's lessons, along with the physical and mental traits and characteristics which were shaped way back in the mists of time by these sadly passed away peoples.

We stand at a pivotal point and moment in the history of us a race of beings. We can make the choice to give this life all that we have and are capable of, therefore heralding the rich and life encrusted baton that holds the ancestry of our very inception and creation. Guaranteeing that what we have, hold and know, will ultimately be passed on fully to those who will come after we have all ceased to be and have joined the vast swathes of deceased beings, fondly termed and known as the ancestors.

Ensuing lives will come and flow, this we know, yet we are all responsible and it is a necessity to instil and imbue the next generation with the skills that are vital to their existence and containment within the same peripherals of love, freedom and enjoyment with which we have all known, shared in and had gifted to us by those who have gone before. The knowledge, along with the richness in all creation is what will guarantee that the next people who are conceived, gifted life and are placed into this beautiful world will thrive and coexist. It is our very core that lies within us, therefore it is cardinal that we grant them the best possible life, leaving them with a vastly rich testimony that will be a resounding corroboration between all our ancestors who have gone before, including ourselves, once our own personal demise happens.

The tides which remonstrate the ebb and flow of creation and life, which epitomise totally and wholly, also encompass and encapsulate just who we are and where we have arrived from are so strong now; we can sense, almost see and touch our ancestors, unlike and unparalleled to any previous times in the history of mankind.

Never before have records shown us just how our individual branches of 'The Tree Of Life' are, allowing us all to allocate, within a plethora of past souls and beings just how the journey to now began and manifested. Discoveries have always been made, although now with the new and giant steps that science has made, we can cast new light and not only estimate the ages and dates of these frequently unearthed discoveries, tombs and bodies, also where they were from, how they died and what they ate while they were alive, then furthering this brilliance with piecing the skeletal remains back together and making lifelike resemblances of how they looked. All of this is nothing short of miraculous and piece by piece and stepping stone by stepping stone, we are allowed and granted the knowledge to actually walk in their footsteps, basically reliving the lives that they along with multiple others and whole communities would have lived as a whole.

Never before has so much progress been accomplished and achieved and if we glance back through the mists of time, we can see vast areas of the time scale which more or less stood still with not a lot happening, nor being achieved apart from survival.

The Tree of Life we are allowed with ease to view today, shows and guides us carefully along the branches and paths that were weaved and forged by the ancestors. Our ancestry and lineage and all of these precious souls were once alive, just as we all are now. It is their lives, along with the great gifts they have left us that will stand us in good stead and assist us in all that we are, do and strive to be. We have been left an incredible legacy and now we are understanding it intricately, showing us further that those who lived recently and within the seemingly dim and distant past, are now being lit up and brought back to life once again, thanks to science and our very inner thirst and desire to know, understand and connect with all that we have been and stemmed from. It is in this understanding, that we can cast light upon exactly who we are now as well as making inner changes which can lead the new generations to a much easier comprehension of how we arrived here. Before we leave this life to continue the constant journey and evolution of our inner selves, we really must take the time and energy to gift these newly arrived souls with the great and timeless gifts that have been bestowed upon us. For within all these artefacts and findings, there is the key to survival, not just ours but also that of the universe and all creation and life that is contained within it. A timeless legacy, that even though now deceased, stands immortalised within the earth's crust waiting to be discovered and analysed, along with museums and vaults around the world. As the ancestors of tomorrow, we simply have to leave a legacy which shows the journey we have all been on.

A proud world stands here now, along with over 7 billion inhabitants, however we live, wherever we live, regardless of race, colour, religious views and beliefs, we should all be immensely proud of who we are and where we have originally stemmed from. If we take a look at ourselves within this vast arena, we should ask ourselves, what part are we playing in the grand scale of life? A balance that provides the inevitable backdrop is quite simply made up of opposing forces, good and bad, wet and dry, dark and light, along with life and death. Without this often underestimated and extremely precarious balance which exists throughout the Universe then all life as we know it could not exist. Therefore what we as individuals may deem as wrong, then in turn cast aspersions and judgements upon, quite simply to make ourselves self important is totally unacceptable and only aids to fuel the ego of the self. We have within our own lives maybe done things that can be seen as wrong, whereas others only appear to do right, it is this harmonious balance that is essential and pivotal to us all and creation as we know it.

The richly imbued tapestry of life is being embroidered constantly and with each separate stitch there are lessons to learn. It is these individual stitches that leave longer strands upon the tapestry and so long as we all learn from our own personal mistakes and then make the predetermined choice to not repeat them, yet learn from them, then the judgements should only remain within ourselves, which we can rectify personally and then put to good use and positivity.

A very wise woman once said to me, 'We are the masters of our own destiny and within that, we have a choice. We are responsible for our own actions, nobody else and we choose whether we create who and what we are, or whether we destroy ourselves.' This is a very powerful statement and understanding, one which I often refer back to and use myself to my friends.

Quite simply, if we liken each thought and action to the singular stitches within the tapestry of life, what would we like to sew into it and be remembered for once we wane, cease to be and become the ancestors of tomorrow?

Our inner souls know exactly what is right and wrong, it's a base make up within us. Admittedly, at times, the boundaries can appear to merge, which leads to doubt and then we can act something out that is totally and morally wrong. Once again, it's all part of the bigger picture and up to us, nobody else, as individuals to harm, which is destroying, or we can decide to create, which is much better all round. This shows that within stitching our own threads into our own personal tapestry of life, we are adding to and making the infinite and much greater tapestry of creation even larger. Then we have to ask ourselves the question, 'What do we want to be known and remembered for?'

As guardians of the magnificent ancestral baton that we now hold and has been left to us, we have made discoveries that only last century, would have appeared as impossible and totally unachievable. However, imbued and instilled with all of the previously discovered and unearthed knowledge which we have been gifted with, we as a people made the choice to recognise and realize just where and how we came into being, simply because we had been left the tools to do so, by the accumulation of remnants, ideas and gathered collective knowledge which our forefathers had left and bequeathed to us.

Like an ethereal relay race, each new generation is handed and then passes on the invisible baton to continue the journey of Mankind. Endowed with wisdom gathered throughout eternity and collected from innumerable sources and beings, we now stand at a precipice in time and as a collective group and consciousness, we have to make that choice, what do we as a race want to be known for, remembered for and etched into time as having done and changed?

We are at a cusp of greatness now, as individuals and as a species, with all the various forms and sources we have readily available and at our disposal. We have the very power to change, shape and mould the whole world and within that we hold the keys to change and make better the lives of millions of people.

Take a bit of time to glance over your shoulder and marvel at the incalculable legions and bastions of all those who have been birthed since the dawning of time and the very emergence of humanity as a species. We would not and could not, be as we are now, and we certainly would not be living as we do without the great sacrifices they made and gave. We owe each one of them an incomprehensible amount of credit and for this life we are in their debt. We now can show them just how grateful we are, we can all pool together as a mass, take a stand and create a world which they have all strived for. Yet it stands with us now, each one of us to come together and manifest exactly what it is we would like to see and have envisaged the world to be once we have passed away and become the ancestors of tomorrow.

The birthing of a new time and age is up to us now, the conceptions and idealistic views which so many have dreamed of in times gone by. We can now make that shift and create a much better and more harmonious home and place to live, along with being known as the generation which changed the world for the better.

We can implement huge changes, we have the knowledge from the tools gifted to us and we have the advancements within science and technology. It is up to us to end famine, to ensure every mouth is fed well and has access to fresh and clean water always. We have the information to stop wars that rage, fighting that ensues and carnage that is left from all of these actions. It is vital that we implement a positive change across the globe. We need to leave a richer and far more contented and peaceful world. We owe this not only to the long lines of ancestry; we also owe it to those who will one day take our place. This has never been done before, yet we have all the strengths, Universal knowledge and technology to make this happen and when we look at what we have achieved, this really is a proverbial drop in the ocean.

What a baton to pass on to those who will be treading these lands after we have gone, an amazing testimony and one which would ensure our parts within the richly embroidered tapestry of life. Let us come together and make a stand, for it is up to us all as individuals to want to make that change, rather than worrying about what we are leaving behind, let us make a conscious decision to become the best that we can, which will have the effect of manifesting with pure intent, just what we would like to see in the world before we leave it behind.

Is it fair on the next generation to still be having to stamp out and extinguish the long burning fires which we might not have lit, but have helped fuel, often through our own ignorance and avoidance of getting down to what truly matters in this life.? It has to stop with us, we are the guardians of all that has been and will be for many years to come. It is crucial now to make that change, then we can pass away peacefully and in the full knowledge that we did our best, utilised all the tools we had been gifted with and had left to us, which will make sure that the generations yet to come, can be proud when they look back and trace their ancestry lineage and discover us, the ancestors of tomorrow.

Walking the Ancestral Road

A RICHLY IMBUED, extremely intricate and wondrous road of ancestry and ancestors has been crafted and forged since time began. The records which are there, showing us the past and those who created our present, along with our future are strewn around and have stamped their place throughout history. They are delicately laid there for us all to explore, devour and to indulge in and connect with, if we choose to, totally.

Never before has all this incredible and highly factual knowledge been so readily available, a magnificent plethora of identification to the past and those who made sure we have a life now is there to be investigated, unlocked and discovered. Whether that is our direct ancestry and lineage, or the culminated ancestors who created the shaping and moulding of the world around us and us as a species.

To start on the more personal journey of unlocking our own lineage couldn't be easier. Family photographs are always a great starting point and from this, the passion and curiosity may well just be the starting point of an amazing journey into our own past, slowly searching and pulling apart our individual heritage and direct blood lines from which we have emerged.

Infinite records have been compiled and literally are there for us all to look through and search with relative ease and once started on this journey it is up to us as to how far we choose, or wish to delve into them. Secrets that have been kept and stored throughout time and millennia, are suddenly not so secret and are gently asking us to look upon and into the journey that has led us to this point in time, who we are and where we have travelled from.

Most towns across the world will have an office where the registration of births, deaths and marriages have been logged and recorded for hundreds of years. If you choose to start your ancestors journey this way, these are a great starting point and can help you compile a very thorough and diversified base level of the journey. From this point, you can start to unravel the intricate threads that have been woven through out time by those who created the rich tapestry of your own and individual lineage.

To actually hold copies of your family's records truly is incredible and extremely humbling. This takes on another concept of connection; reading and seeing their signatures, warming to the touch and resonating within your psyche on a much deeper and intrinsic level. This brings us so close to them all, sensing the happiness at a recorded birth, the elation of a long gone family marriage and the sheer loss and void that is apparent from a death. Within all this, you are connecting so closely with them all, you are bringing the memories back to life, which in a sense brings those people, our families, back to life. However distant and brief this may seem, that is what is happening.

For a fairly nominal fee, it is possible to join one of the many ancestry sites which are available online and literally, at the touch of a button, we can connect with those sacred souls who have left this world yet ensured that we will have life and these ancestors who have helped build up our own Tree of Life, are reaching out to us from beyond the veil, encouraging and beckoning us onto a journey which will guide and show us the many multitudes of beings which our personal paths have stemmed from, strayed from and all encompassing together, creating the rich and decadent lives which the majority of us have and ultimately lead now.

Once we have taken the proverbial plunge into this infinite pool of ancestry, we are bringing the past to life, effectively breathing new life and energy into those beings and souls who left this life many years before. Yet with this new technology, our understanding and unbounded records which have been forged through time, we can unlock the past, gifting breathe into those who have delivered us to this point. A key fact in this journey is the amazing combination of records and events which have been recorded and kept for posterity through the ages, which were seemingly obscured throughout time. Hand written forms, scrawled notes and passages on parchment papers, all kept, because it was important to do so. Yet now, with our instant access to these priceless paper records, we culminate the past with the present on our screens to transform archaic, distant records, almost lost over the years. We can now, instantly again, print them off, rekindling and restoring those lives that have been deceased and gone for many, many years.

Treading the path and searching the various complex and innumerable steps which lead us deep into the very roots of our ancestry is nothing short of an incredulous journey, full of surprises, remarkable discoveries and for many there will be shocks, maybe even heartbreak along the way. It is true that, as individuals and as a race, we are, or should, be all moving forwards. Another take on this is that the past is in the past for a reason. There are those that state, it should remain that way. I personally believe that there is so much that we can learn from this magical journey. Many stones will be and need to be overturned. Without undertaking this sacred journey, we cannot understand, nor acknowledge where we have come from. If we don't know where or how we have arrived at this point in time, then how can we derive just who we are and where we could be heading? As with any decision we make, it is so easy to arrive and face conundrums along the way. Yet to gain an astute and higher perception of exactly who we are, why we live where we do, the personal traits and characteristics that we each have and portray as individuals, then it is definitive to us all that we carefully unpick and unstitch the many layers of invisible threads that have been woven into the rich and very decorative tapestry that forms the base line to who we are, how we came to be here now, along with every person that played a part in our arrival and conception. We owe it to ourselves to unwrap the tightly entwined branches of the very tree that has shaped itself over many thousands of years and look within the very trunk of that Tree, which is our lineage, our ancestry and which will inevitably help us to understand all the distinctive and personalised traits, along with the eccentricities which we all carry and have instilled deep within us. Our own ancestry and lineage, along with the collective of generalised ancestors have fed and fuelled the sparks which ignited constantly along the way and through the countless generations before us. We owe it all of these souls to realise, discover and let their story be told, for each one has a very definitive tale to tell. It is up to us now to rekindle those vast swathes of life, now deceased, and to let their voices roar with the lessons and invaluable knowledge that they each have to pass onto us.

Once we start this journey, there is a very high chance (the same with anything really that we choose to do and are passionate about) that when we scratch the surface, we may well become almost consumed by this highly pleasurable and vastly interesting quest which we have undertaken and find ourselves on.

Recently departed relatives are just the tip of this infinite iceberg and from this; a very special journey will ultimately begin. The family trees are immeasurable, so a good way to start, is to trace existing members of the family. From this we can actually make contact with them. Wherever these individuals live in the world, with relative ease we can track them down. Whether that is from being given their address and making contact that way (social media sites also provide an excellent way of finding people, linking them together) then from that, we can chat online, slowly building up to having phone calls, talking via video links to anywhere in the world. Then it is just a fairly small step to actually visiting, meeting up and embracing members of our own family tree. At this point, the most miraculous journey will start, grow, manifest and flourish. It is up to each one of us to make that first step, then once we do, we slowly yet surely lift the invisible curtains, or veils upon the most fascinating of all stories and adventures, the very one that will see us go back in time, as far as we wish, to discover all those individual and very sacred souls who all played a part in delivering us to this point in time and gifting us with who we are, what we are and all that is contained within us.

The ease of travelling nowadays ensures us that we can visit most places, anywhere in the world really, within 24 hours. Another modern luxury, that at times is so easily taken for granted, yet can prove invaluable to us all.

Never before throughout our history, however far back we look, has anything been so readily welcoming and available to us all, regardless of culture and age restrictions. The past is hailing and welcoming us all to have a look, lift the veil between worlds and step into not just the past, but our long, beautiful and very curious past. A time to utilise all the strewn and discarded remnants of what has gone before in order to create us and the world around us. If we look, we can see clearly the abundance of discoveries, charred remains, bone fragments, whole skeletal remains, tools and weapons unearthed (some dating back thousands of years), buildings that still stand, shrouded with metaphysical footprints and memories from long ago. Plaques and headstones that are set as constant and physical reminders of souls that have gone before, priceless artefacts, minute pieces of pottery, elaborate ornaments, all gifting us keys to the infinite portal of time gone by. If we wish to pick and carefully undo the lock, we can willingly enter a fantastical world which lies beyond our one, yet it is the culmination of all these, plus many more pieces of our past, that constantly reach out and call to us all, to take the first steps into discovering exactly how we came into being, along with breathing life back into these incredible gallant and valiant beings that carved the world around them, gifting us the elaborate jewel encrusted baton that has been bestowed upon not only mankind as a race and species, but each one of us as individuals.

Combine all the actual physical representations of our ancestors with the instant accessibility of researching, and discovering them almost instantly online, then it is easy to see that the shrouds of time that were only to be imagined not that long ago, have suddenly and very apparently, been opened wide for us all to enter into, on quests of ancestors as a wider investigation, or a far more individual and personalised search for those unique beings that moulded our own lineage throughout the ages.

Before this point in time, a lot of speculation was thrown into the mix as to how we came into being and how our separate branches from the tree of life slowly formed, came into being and gradually emerged. This is now not the case, the plethora and infinite amount of factual evidence, physical proof and online confirmation now is astounding. It is there in abundance just waiting to be unwrapped and to momentarily be gifted life once again by us as we search, compile and allow re-emergence of the past into the now.

This is no longer a cabalistic ideology, but proven fact with undoubted and historic evidence that is literally enticing us and prompting us all to open up what was viewed before, as the Pandora's Box of discovery. With the past so open and almost visible to us, in a multitude of various guises, we can now venture out on a hermetic journey which will take us into a glorious world that was built, shaped and formed by an infinite number of extremely beautiful, totally unique and very sacred souls, without whom, we would not be standing here today.

Once we make, should we choose to do so, the decision of walking the Ancestral road, we will find that it opens up to us. Messages are given and shared, new discoveries will be found, hidden names and mysterious links are all there to be found and unearthed and marvelled at. Some will shoot off in other directions, yet they will all provide us with knowledge and will show us just how we came into being and evolved gradually through the ages, slowly emerging through and out of the mists of time.

Personal memorabilia, various antiquities, photographs, books and many other individual artefacts always provide us with a great link to those who have now gone and passed away. These priceless possessions gift us a physical representation and tight link to those whom we have loved and hold dear to us, cherishing the memories that are rich and abundant within our hearts for those we shared parts of our lives with. The significance these various trinkets hold can be invaluable, leaving fond memories engrained upon us like indelible ink as we fondly recall where we first held and saw these treasures, often as young children, as they were all part of the legacy of growing up, whether these riches were in the homes of our parents, who may well have sadly passed away, or other family members who we have lost yet adored and loved beyond reason.

If we look upon and reflect at all the memories we hold deep within our minds and physicality, then we can sense these cherished souls constantly, around us and within all we do and strive to be. It is these echoes of times and people past that, no matter where we go, what we do and what happens, will thankfully never be erased from our memory banks and nor should they be, as without these inner stirrings and connections to who and what has been, we would often and invariably do flounder at some of life's trials. These adoring and unconditional beings that we reciprocate those feelings to, provide us with an anchor that, when life's turbulent seas toss and turn us, often testing us, physically, mentally and spiritually, without knowing, we hold on to their memories. Whether we realise and vocalise it, we are reaching out to them across the realms, simply to seek their guidance, their counsel, asking them for answers and advice. This becomes a natural reaction, something no doubt that we would have done time and time again when they were alive, seeking solace and shelter. Hence the reason we automatically do it, even when we know they have left this mortal earthly coil, our inner being knows deep within that they are still around us and there for us, departed from this life yes, yet we sense, feel and our souls know they are literally only a heartbeat away and still guide and strengthen us constantly, in all that we are and do.

However we envisage those who have passed, our very core and inner beings reach out to them, for they may have departed us in the physical sense of being, yet our hearts know that not only can we transcend other worlds and realms to reach out to them, but also that they often enter into our minds, our being, our hearts and cross through and over from their world into ours. Culminated together, souls connected and tightly forged, entwined for all time, these sacred souls are constantly with us, for not only do we sense them around, we know and can feel them within our very hearts, they spur us on and grant us the fire in our stomachs that gives us the constant drive and encouragement to carry on, often through tough times and adversity. Not only did they gift us life and breath to begin with, they push us on always and are living their lives through us, as all our ancestors are. Once we start to walk the ancestral road, this becomes apparent to us on all of our levels of being and our conscious states.

Dream states are a valuable time for the transference of messages and signs and I have no doubt at all that we have all dreamt about a very cherished family member who sadly is no longer with us, yet still we receive visitations offering various solutions to what can be deemed as trying questions through life. With great simplicity, the answers we were seeking are often expressed and granted to us through these asleep, yet heightened times within a dream like slumber.

Whatever path we follow, whether it is a faith, belief, tradition, or a specified religion, we cannot deny that we are all being guided by those who are no longer here. Yet through the varying states of being, these souls permeate the shrouds and veils that separate the worlds, offering us hope, guidance and an infinite number of other solutions, along with great comfort and strength. Once we undertake the steps to unlock our lineage and discover our past and those who created it, we can sense that we are all tethered together, although by unseen threads. We can see that our lives are inter woven throughout time and however small a part some people may have had to play in our arrival, take nothing away from that, as every part is just as vital as all the other pieces. If you take one fragment away, the whole tale of Ancestry fails, therefore the story could not have possibly worked out as it has done, all of which will become more appreciated and respected the further we walk along this extremely consecrated path that takes us back into and through the past, our past, along with showing us the very magical journey to where we stand now.

Standing on a proverbial precipice of not only our life, but the lives who have handed us the very mantle of birth and freedom to reach this point in time and at this precise moment in all of time, it truly is remarkable and nothing short of miraculous. We hold the knowledge, ways of the past and the technology of today, which, if we incorporate and blend together, the results we can receive are truly mesmerising. The solitary paths which reflect the lone journey taken by each one of our own ancestors can now be bought totally to life, taking the search to a completely new level of understanding, which until now has been beyond comprehension and remained merely within the vivid scopes of imagination, almost illusive. We can now physically enter into the past, breathing life into the long deceased souls who have assisted by playing their parts of mapping out the world, creating infinite chains of life and bought to fruition everything that has been, is now and will be in the future, which includes us and those to come.

To walk the ancestral road is to literally transport ourselves back through the mists of time and connect with those souls who paved the way for our birthing, inception and rise to this point at this time. This is effectively invoking the spirits and ancestors of the past as a salutation to each one of them, paying respect, giving thanks and showing they have not been forgotten and that they won't be left undiscovered, but will be remembered fondly now and for evermore.

Once we start, which is at the beginning, the first step is our most recently departed and deceased family members, which is merely scratching the surface of what will turn into a mystery to be solved. The clues are left there, just waiting for us to find them and piece them all together in what will be the greatest story that has ever been told, the one which forms the solidity and very backbone of how we are here now. The benefits of this are clear to see, without knowing our past and how we have arrived at this point, how can we possibly begin to grasp and understand where we are heading and what the Universe has in store for us?

Recently deceased family members provide us with a firm foundation to work from and several of these we will have known personally, our parents, aunts, uncles, cousins and so on. From this, we can slowly start to unearth and discover the various parts and other shoots which have stemmed and grown. Slowly parting the small branches of our recent ancestors, we can travel farther and farther back, which will inevitably take time and dedication. The more shoots we discover, the thicker the branches become. This is apparent before we even set out and embark on this journey, simply because we know that we have a huge number of beings that gave us this life, therefore the more we look, the more we find. At the end of each branch of ancestry, a thicker, more abundant branch, strewn with many more individuals is there waiting to be found and researched.

This goes on and on, then maybe once we have researched and verified all of these beings, with modern technology moving on so swiftly and new discoveries of defunct life and civilisations that were, we could well be in sight, metaphorically speaking, of making the philosopher's stone discovery of finding out just who started the incredible beginnings of not only our ancestry tree but also the very beginnings of mankind as a species and the race as we know it.

We only have to ponder and reflect upon how quickly we, as a collective have evolved over the last two hundred years. Our intimate and very broad and factual knowledge has gone way beyond anything that was considered, not only as plausible, yet even possible, until fairly recently. Monumental leaps have come to fruition, scientifically, physically, mentally and spiritually. We are all at a point in time where not only is something likely, but highly possible. Evolution and comprehensive understanding have transcended all boundaries that were once in place, yet we now know that anything is achievable and more often than not, it happens very quickly. We see this happening constantly and coming to fruition in our lifetimes.

Conveniently and strategically peppered along the Ancestry road, are all the clues and findings we will need to discover our past and all those unique individuals that slowly and surely, not only helped to shape and create the world around them as they went along their own daily lives, but formed the immense, almost incalculable and vast swathes of life, all of which are tightly interwoven and embroidered, strand by strand and thread by thread into the most elaborate, picturesque and most wondrous tale and story that has ever been told, the very story that shows us who, how and why we as a race have existed so long, made the giant leaps forward and gifted all of us, with the strength, clarity, wisdom and vast knowledge that we now have at our disposal.

The richly encrusted baton of history has been handed to each one of us. It is up to us to treasure it totally, respect all those sacred souls who have played a part in its deliverance to us at this time and also to show the greatest respect to all those who bore it before, by gifting them life once again, rekindling the fires that burn so bright in all life and walk the path of Ancestry, slowly unfurling the many and various branches that have come slowly to fruition, grown and evolved to bequeath us this life that we have now in all its wondrous beauty.

Ancestry within Cultures Around the World

THE VARIOUS CELEBRATIONS that are held around the world within different cultures, faiths, beliefs and traditions are widely diversified. The common goal though, is to connect and honour all those beings that have passed away, leaving us with their legacy and special memories to cherish and hold sacred within us.

Within the Celtic tradition, which has its roots embedded across much of Western Europe, the time of celebrating the dead is the 31st October – 1st November. This time is seen as the time when the veil that separates this world from the realm of the deceased is at its thinnest, almost invisible, so contact and communication between both parties is when it is at its easiest and most heightened, a very special time indeed. Known and referred to as Samhain by those who celebrate the Celtic tradition and, nowadays, by those who prefer some of the various branches of pagan traditions, including the neo-pagan belief systems.

A multitude of ways in which to celebrate this most sacred of times within the ever moving and constant wheel of the year can be seen and joined in with. These can range from having a photo of a special loved one, to holding a physical ceremony to invoke and manifest the spirits of long gone ancestors. Representations of dead souls can be put in place. Again, these can range from artefacts, pictures, even apples in many cases, all of which can make it easier to see a physical object, giving focus and strength to call upon them, honour and worship their passing, the lives they had and the importance which they have within our lives and society today.

As time has moved on, a lot of these age old and almost timeless traditions have become diluted somewhat, also adopted within other beliefs and religious ceremonies. Samhain is one of these and it was in and around the 5th and 6th centuries that this most sacred of times was adopted by the Christian belief, who had their interpretation endorsed upon it and it is from this that 'All Hallows Eve,' or Halloween came about.

The time and true meaning of Samhain has over the last few decades seen a resurgence once again, thanks to the various strains of the pagan and neo-pagan beliefs, which is fantastic to see and be a part of, taking us back into a time when life and death were more natural, celebrated and honoured totally, without any ulterior motives and the sad commercialism factor that is prevalent in today's modernistic way of life.

The Buddhist way of life celebrates this time and it is known as 'Obon.' Seen as the time when the Spirits of their Ancestors return to their homes and partake in the lives that they once had. This time of remembrance and celebration happens during July in Japan and in August in China, which is more to do with the individual take on the solar calendar than anything else. Often seen as an oppressive and fairly dark time of celebration, as with many times in which the deceased are remembered and honoured, Obon is anything but dark. Celebrations are widespread, food and drink is shared within small groups and large villages and towns join in these festivities together. Often clothing is worn that is very brightly coloured, fires and lanterns are lit, all to show reverence and respect to those individuals who have passed through the veil that separates worlds, are no longer with us. Yet they are never forgotten and are remembered and celebrated fondly at these times of the year.

Dia de los Muertos (The Day of the Dead) is known around the world, not necessarily for the celebrations, but the associations around and within this time of celebrating. The elaborate and very decadent skull shapes that appear and are known around the world, termed as 'Sugar Skulls,' are a massive part of these celebrations.

Celebrated throughout Latin America and closely linked with Mexico, the Day of the Dead is a huge two day festival, which brings together swathes of neighbouring villages, towns, cities and countries. Large festivities involve an almost Carnival-like atmosphere, with processions, dancing, singing, eating, drinking and much revelry.

Tombs and graves are adorned with photographs and flowers. One of the most popular physical representations is bread, which is often cooked and shaped to resemble piles of bones. These are often placed onto the graves and altars to honour the deceased.

The Carnival atmosphere continues with skeletons, skull and bone shapes being portrayed in abundance everywhere, from the clothing and make up worn, right through to the Carnival floats, cars and posters displayed for all to see. Flowers and bright colours are also used as another way to show respect and give honour to the ancestors.

From the smallest, almost primitive Islands that live plainly, sweeping through the multitude of various communities, villages and towns that are festooned around the world, incorporating an infinite number of beliefs, religions and ways of being, regardless of what belief structure is enforced, or held, we all have our own ways of acknowledging, paying respect to and honouring our Ancestors and all those precious souls who have gone before, leaving us with memories, however distant and the very legacy that is the lives we live and enjoy today.

Communing with the Ancestors

OFTEN SEEN AS an almost dark art and practice, communing with the deceased and our ancestors is still largely viewed as a very taboo subject, especially within the Western societies that many of us live in. The fact is that all cultures and all beliefs around the world have been built on messages and symbols from the past. Therefore, communication and practical hindsight has been used to build upon what we have learnt and witnessed from those who are now passed away. Effectively we have used the messages they left us.

I find it fascinating and rather strange really that people will willingly go and visit trance mediums, clairvoyants and various seers and openly ask them to be a conduit to bridge the gap between our physical world and the realm of the dead, hoping to find answers and signs from the deceased. Yet within the mainstream of society, this is still to this day a revered topic of conversation.

Whichever cultural group we have been born into, whatever our beliefs and wherever we may live within the world, our ancestors and the deceased in general have left and continue to leave us signs constantly. Whether that is in symbolism form within the physical sense, or within messages that can often manifest within the ethereal realms, we are communing with them constantly and on a daily basis.

As we gaze back throughout history, we can easily see and visit buildings that were constructed by our ancestors (I am using the term ancestors as a collective, not necessarily as a direct, or specific lineage). From these magnificent structures, we can learn so much; materials used, methods of building, tools used and so on. Therefore, we can learn from these physical world representations so much and culminate all that is on view widely around us to benefit and strengthen our own lives and possible future buildings that may well be in plan. From the ships that have sailed throughout time, the paths and roadways we travel upon, the houses we dwell and live in, the intricate ways we undertake certain tasks, the way we talk, view different aspects of life and all that is contained within this beautiful world and Universe, all of this is a culmination of messages that have been left by those who have lived before us and are now permanent fixtures within the landscapes of physicality, as well as the realms of our own minds, stamped like indelible ink and etched within the mists of time.

During our sleep time, the time when our physical bodies are recharging which is an extremely powerful time; our minds assess and compartmentalise the various experiences we have had during the previous day as well as sorting out what has happened during our lives. Effectively working like a computer and putting separate folders in place, which makes it easier to recall and remember the plethora of aspects and experiences that we have contained within us all as individual beings.

Sleep time is one of the most powerful mediums that there are and it is often during this time when communing with our departed loved ones and our Ancestry as a whole comes into being. This is a two way thing as during these times, not only do they approach and enter our dream state to pass on and gift us with messages and insights, we also call them to us, conjuring up thoughts and invoking them to come and converse with us.

The hypothesis of communication is often seen as the mainstream mediums of talking directly, or vocalisation and reading. The fact is though, that these ways of communication play only a very small part in how we interact with one another. Intentionally or not, we are contacting and responding constantly to everybody, whether we are aware of this, or even actually think about it, we are. Around 93% of all communication is non verbal. Which shows us that basically we are antennas transmitting constantly within the multitude of varying mediums. These can range from a smile and a nod, to how we walk and conduct ourselves, whether we give eye contact, the clothes we choose to wear on different days, the stance we take when standing, the list is endless. What it comes down to though, is that we are all able to sense and articulate how we feel about and are to one another, because at the core of our very being; we are all energy and it is this non visual energy that gifts us life and makes us who we are and act as we do.

As our physical bodies are resting and at sleep, it is during this time when our energy or spiritual self transcends into different and various realms and journeys into other worlds that are not so prominent and as easily accessible to most people while they are awake and functioning in their day to day lives.

The understanding and recognition of communication whilst asleep is imperative simply to comprehend that messages can be and are frequently transmitted and received between ourselves and our Ancestors during this time.

If we make the comparison of our sleep state to being in a trance, much like the various Mediums and Clairvoyants that many openly seek and are prepared to pay money to, then it is easier to get a grip on it, simply because we are all capable of communing with the deceased, especially when in our sleep state.

We often awake with positivity, vibrancy and overwhelming feelings of contentment and inner clarity, at times we have no idea why we feel this way, then we can often receive a physical sign, maybe hear music, read an article, or overhear a conversation, then we instantly recall and remember a particular dream we may have had, then it all becomes much clearer and we then can recognise and interpret the dream, the intricacies of it, the realisation and full picture of what happened, what was meant and who we were communicating with at that time.

The world in which we live and carry out our daily lives in is full of other realms. We only have to look around us to envisage this. The ancient monuments that adorn our lands, the primitive cave paintings and etched carvings that have been discovered, the graves, written historical facts, buildings that many of us live in, music we listen to frequently, right through to how we look, those we resemble and our inner traits and mannerisms. Symbols, signs and messages all contributing to the fact that we are all a part of one another and we are each inexplicably linked to those who have gone before, countless numbers of souls who lived recently, as well as many hundreds, even thousands of years ago, all culminating with those individuals who we now call our ancestors.

We have all arrived here from the same source, that source being the Universe as a whole, so to imagine and realise that we are all as one, all equal and closely linked, is simple to comprehend and it is from this very point that to understand that we are all communicating on a very base and primeval level, is indeed part of our makeup and core essence.

There are many times when we can feel alone, lost almost and in need of comfort and reassurance, we have all felt these feelings and emotions, I know I have. Often at times like this, I have felt immensely comforted, soothed, cradled even with overwhelming feelings of positivity and love that quickly ensue. For me personally there is only one answer to this, my loved ones are reaching out and giving me comfort and strength from beyond the veil that separates our world from theirs, the Ancestors are visiting me and easing me through whatever tough times I may be having.

Whatever our own personal take on these signs and messages may be, we cannot dismiss that there is a world much greater than the one we live in within our physical bodies and world. To even try to or contemplate that this is it and there is nothing else falls short totally and to deny this is to deny the past. Therefore we are casting doubts on our ancestors, our very lineage and ourselves, simply because without the past, there can be no present.

The world in which we live is made up and intricately stitched with the fine threads of time, our own lineage, those of all living beings and those who have lived, toiled, endured and existed since time began. We are living in the conclusion of all of this as it is the now. That conclusion though, never ends, it carries on from generation to generation. Each moment is an ending and each moment is a new beginning, it is up to us how we use it and how we choose to act within it. However we choose to be, there is no getting away from the core fact that we are all as one, whether that is in our awake time, or dream state of slumber. The constant relaying of individual and wider scoped messages we can view, see, feel, smell and sense on all our levels of consciousness and subconciousness, is undeniable, it comes down to our acceptance of it all.

Communing with those who sadly are no more is part of our base makeup and DNA and it happens with regularity. How we choose to listen and interpret this communication is up to us as individuals. To listen and sense is key here, as our ancestors have lived before; they know and are much more attuned to the highs, lows and inner workings of all life and creation, therefore they have all the answers that we seek. Listen to them, learn, grow and evolve from the personalised lessons that they are willing to teach us, it's just in a different format and context, now that they have passed away. They have now left this mortal coil, yet the messages they relay to us are much appreciated and a great guidance and comfort to us.

Invoking the Ancestors

INVOCATION CAN BE bought about in a wide array and multitude of different ways. From the moment we first wake each morning, whether we are aware of the fact, or oblivious to it, we are effectively summoning those we have loved and who sadly are no longer with us, to invigorate, strengthen and accompany us on our journey through each day.

We all contain singular strands of our direct lineage plus the infinite and vast threads of not only our ancestors, but ancestry as a whole collective. Therefore we are imbued with them from our very conception. This is obvious and par for the course, hence while we are living and breathing, we are effectively living our lives not just for us, but also for vast swathes of all the sacred beings that have walked and lived before us and have put their mark upon us. It is these precious souls that, as well as the wider Universe, we stir within our core being once we awake and arrive into each new day.

Accompanied in the spiritual sense by legions of ancestors that date back to the inception of time, we are all walking with our Ancestors. Through the unseen threads that make up the invisible web of life, which covers all of creation, all realms and all beings, we are never alone. The manifestation of these individuals is, for most of the time, totally unseen. Yet if we are aware then we can feel and sense them all around and within us constantly. As living beings we are the epitome of all life that has been. For that reason, we are invoking the memories, thoughts and patterning of all creation, stirring them with our actions, our thoughts, our minds. Within all this, we are asking for comfort, guidance, insight, wisdom and strength.

Regardless of deity beliefs, cultural traditions and the different religions or paths we hold dear and may follow, there is no escaping that however small the summoning may be, or seem, we all at some time invoke, in the physical sense the spirits of our loved ones and the souls of our ancestors. These various callings can be seen and heard in countless different ways, many of them are mainstream and can often be done without thinking. In a sense, we remain oblivious to the actual realisation of what we are doing; which is summoning up, or invoking the spirits of the deceased. However we view this interpretation, that is what we are doing and all of us do it, some knowingly, many unknowingly and unwittingly, it's the same however we see it.

The sad fact is that to openly admit we are communing with the dead is still a very revered topic and one that within a lot of the Western world is still a taboo subject, shied away from and almost frowned upon, unless you are an accepted medium or clairvoyant the wider world tends to view you with much criticism and cynicism. It is clear to see that we all at some time undertake and practice this, so here are a few of the ways in which we invoke the Ancestors and these are easily recognisable.

Prayer is probably the most known form of invocation and it is used, in its various forms, around the world and within all religious beliefs, traditions and faiths across all cultures. Within the prayer, there is often very deep, almost meditative thought. So whether we just peruse this in our minds, or further this process with vocalisation, humming, singing, or chanting, what we are actually doing is performing the timeless method of releasing our inner incantation. Calling upon and out to, summoning and invoking the Universe and all that is contained within, more often than not, it is our departed loved ones and ancestors whilst undertaking this practice. I believe that prayer, personalised salutation, incantation, blessing, however we choose to term it, is the most powerful way in which we can make a direct link and pledge to those who have gone before us and are sadly now deceased. Starting with our own internalised thought process, we begin to awaken ourselves spiritually, which in itself is calling out beyond our physical world. This then transcends through the veil that separates worlds, almost like sending an early signal out in preparation to whoever we may be asking and calling out to.

To further strengthen this we often say the prayer thought and in doing so, it becomes hugely cathartic, cleansing and extremely invigorating. What we are actually doing is releasing our hopes, fears, dreams, pains, love and a whole multitude of pent up feelings and emotions. Unless we actually choose, or designate the party, or parties (as in various deities we are drawn to, or favoured ancestors) we are giving and putting our thoughts within the prayer straight to the source of the universe. Which from where, be it instantly, or over an unscheduled period of time, we do receive answers, comfort and messages. It's up to us as individuals as to how we choose to acknowledge, accept and take them on board.

Prayer is totally universal and can be used in a plethora of ways and there is no designated structure to it. We can pray in our heads on our own, we can then take the further step of releasing it vocally whilst alone, or within larger groups. There is no right or wrong way to pray, there is no set time and we can undertake this most sacred of acts wherever we are and whenever we choose to do so.

To communicate through the medium of prayer is undoubtedly the best form of direct contact we can undertake to reach our ancestors and departed loved ones. It needs no fabric, as such, and can be viewed as a lament to the powers that be. Often we can and do invariably talk out loud, even when alone. This is a further analogy of inner thoughts and prayers simply being released outwardly. Whatever we say and think, the words are heard and felt, resonating to those intended, whether they are living or not.

Once we know, sense and feel that our words during prayer are being heard and answered we can begin to strengthen the fabric on which our prayers are based and outwardly vocalised. This alone brings about a huge shift within our realisation, an awakening spiritually that endorses the beliefs we hold inside. Not only are we reaching out to the deceased, but also they hear us, answer us and will often act and aid us in whatever form is fitting, whether that may be a subtle message just to us, or through direct answer.

It is from this point that we know, beyond the shadow of any doubts, that invocation and the summoning up of our ancestors is apparent and does happen, undeniably. As long as we are pure in our thoughts, mindful, aware and show respect, along with honour to them constantly and there is no malice, ill thought, or ulterior motives, then for the majority of the time when we ask, we are answered, comforted. Solace of the self can be found and achieved through the sacred act of prayer.

Meditation is another form of being able to allow interactions between worlds to flow freely and is another extremely powerful medium of communication and invocation between ourselves and our Ancestors.

During this time, our physical being basically switches off.

Our minds stop thinking and we become clear of thoughts that invade our day to day lives. We stop being, therefore the receiving and transmitting of messages becomes heightened as our subconscious self starts to stir and awaken as it is now alleviated of all the normal life processes that can restrict and impede us. Whilst we are in these trance-like states of meditation, what we become is a totally open conduit; in effect communication with the deceased can flow freely during these times. To understand this further, we only have to look towards other cultures Witch Doctors and wise people regularly undertake and enter meditative states in order to approach and ask the spirit world for guidance and clarity. Native American tribes use meditation to seek answers for a multitude of questions, ranging from wars, the weather, where to plant crops and where to relocate to. Termed and known more widely now as shamans, the action and operation is still the same, has stood the test of time and is appreciated as a direct link in the invocation of the ancestors and the realm of the dead.

Dance can also be used and frequently is, as a way of communing with the deceased. Stirring the timeless spirits of old and re-enacting some of the dances that have been around and used for in numerous ways.

Many tribes around the world have their own designated way of dancing to invoke the ancestors and these are often used and displayed in times of possible war, which summons up powers of protection and guidance, along with stimulating and empowering the soldiers who are ultimately performing the age old traditions of the dance.

Rain dances are another commonly seen of way of invoking the deceased as well as other deities that may be called upon, carried out to enhance the tribes', or communities' crops. Hoping and directly asking for abundance from the soil and the seeds that have been planted, all to ensure health and longevity for the whole tribe in question.

One of the many dances that invokes the spirits of the ancestors that the majority of us will have heard of and possibly seen is performed with regularity by the New Zealand rugby team, the All Blacks. The Haka is an age old war cry or dance that has its origins and foundations firmly rooted within the Maori people of New Zealand within the Southern Hemisphere. It is this dance, which appears quite intimidating that calls upon the ancestors and invokes the spirits, like a call to arms and directly asks for the summoning up of strength and courage from those who are now deceased and no more. Yet through the veil that separates worlds, open communication and invigoration is sought and mustered.

The lighting and significance of burning candles is another medium that can be seen on display across the world, yet is often overlooked and not directly associated with the invocation of the deceased and our much loved ancestors.

The very act of lighting a candle shows a mark of respect and within this, the mind and thought process behind it, is a symbol of recognition. More often than not, candles are used to provide inner peace, warmth and clarity and are also closely linked with the ritual that accompanies prayer.

Fire is one of the main base elements that make up the Universe along with being contained within all life and creation. Within its containment, fire provides us with life, warmth, protection and many other sources that aid us immensely in our daily lives. To harness this element safely, which is what we do each time we light a candle, is to invigorate our whole being. Gifting us with soothing mental stimulation, a physical manifestation that gives us focus and an inner spiritual clarity, which, when combined together, gives us feelings of inner and outer peace, warmth, strength, subtly imbued power and heightened awareness of all our senses.

Providing inner solace and contentment, as well as stimulation to our very core being, a flickering flame and the soothing light that emanates from it also transcends and permeates through the shroud that separates worlds. This is well known and is effective via and from both parties, whichever side they happen to be on and reside within.

Unleashed, fire can be deadly and totally devastating. Yet the humble candle which, when lit, has the totally opposite effect and beautiful resonations of soothing comfort are felt deep within and right through to our ethereal spirits and souls which epitomise just who and what we are. Forging another conduit or way of expressing our heartfelt emotions, fears and sorrows, as well as the pure love and joy we feel inside. It is all these sentiments that we can freely express and show, both physically and metaphysically, each time we light the sacred candle.

One of the effects and uses of fire is to purify and cleanse and this can clearly be seen, as well as felt once a fire is lit, be it a large fire, or a much smaller version that is apparent in the dancing naked flame of a candle.

Renowned the world over and used within mainstream cultures, beliefs and life, the symbolism of candles is applauded and has been for thousands of years. Used in a whole host of various ways, it is more often than not used as a sign of remembrance, whether that is to mark a birthday, a death, anniversaries, to give thanks or a myriad of other celebratory times and events.

Often combined with prayer the candle then takes on a much deeper meaning and this can be viewed around the globe, especially at times of immense loss and bereavement, tragedy and heartache when people, whole communities and countries at times, unite together to express their own and inner deep sorrows, yet find comfort and some peace by the manifestation of joining together and uniting in grief by praying, using candles as a focus. All of this combined is in effect, a way of reaching out to and invoking the spirits and souls of the ancestors.

Music and singing are other powerful mediums that can be used to reach out and totally connect with the powers that be, universally as in tapping into the direct source of all life and creation, also making contact with the ancestors. Since the earliest human type beings had evolved enough to hold sticks, I don't think there can be any doubt that at times of melancholy and joy, these sticks would have been tapped, or banged against an object creating a very simple and basic drumming sound, which over time would have become elaborated and rhythmical.

Music, however simple it may seem resonates deep within us. Especially a constant banging like that of a drum, replicating the heart beat that lies within us all as well as throughout all creation, stirring our very essence and immediately transporting us back to the most sacred of places where we have all come from, the feminine womb and before that, the womb of the universe, from where we all originate and were born out of.

Invigorating our very being music energises us and can lift our spirits totally, almost to a place and state of deep meditation, enraptured with the harmonious sounds and frequencies that are being emitted. It is very similar to a trance like state, or higher conscious level of heightened stimulation. Ethereal basically, and reaching into other realms and worlds, much like our ancestors would have done throughout time.

Undeniably music is another great medium and provides a further contact with the spirit world, the place where our dearly departed loved ones and the ancestors throughout time now reside.

Transcending in and out of our physical world and penetrating through the veil and into other realms is all about invocation and summoning, stirring ourselves and the Ancestors to forge a mutual appreciation and show respect, harmoniously and with heightened love and adoration.

Singing is a huge release and we all do it, whether we are able to vocalise or not, we still sing. Maybe in our heads, or humming, these are all ways in which we can reach out. Half the time we don't know we are actually doing it, we just do, another almost primeval way of communicating even when we have nobody to communicate with.

Throughout history and time, songs have been put together and created, shouted, sung, whistled, spoken and hummed and it is through these intense and beautiful melodic vocalisations that have often been used the world over as a way to show respect and love, we can directly summon up and conjure together the very spirits of the ancestors.

Singing is a way in which we can rejoice, bring people together, harmonise and spread powerful messages. To sing is to tap into the source of creation and in doing this, we automatically connect with everything and everyone, past and present, invocation again and connecting with the spirits of the old and those now deceased.

Ethereal and melodic singing is a beautiful way to express ourselves, to stimulate and heighten our levels of consciousness. Ultimately, in doing this, we become transported away into another realm of being. Stimulating and extremely arousing songs and words have been sung and chanted throughout time as a way to directly invigorate and stir the physical self. War chants and cries came into being as a direct way of imbuing the ancestors before entering battles and dangerous situations, fighting, going to war and hunting prey. Within these chants, protection, strength, speed, bravery, tenacity and a whole array of other traits would be, and still are, asked for, being imbued and gifted the ways and wisdom of those who have done it before many years ago, ultimately; the ancestors.

Once we combine instrumental music and accompany it with vocalised singing, then we are strengthening the very essence of the songs we sing, much the same as using a candle with the medium of prayer, they each complement one another, stimulate us on a much deeper level of being, therefore we can be more focused, purer and heightened totally, This allows us to invoke and connect with all the powers that be and the ancestors on a much deeper and intrinsic level.

There are many different methods we can utilise to connect with our departed loved ones and the ancestors as a wider collective. From the simplest of day to day tasks which we undertake and perform, some may be ritualistic, whereas some we do without actually thinking or acknowledging the action.

Whether we pray in some way, say a daily mantra or affirmation, empower ourselves with a dance or song, we might meditate, light candles with regularity, or we may well seek personal solace at a loved one's graveside, or frequently visit a place that was their favoured spot, it doesn't matter. In all of these ways, whether as part of a larger group, or independently, what we are actually doing, again unknowingly, is taking the time to connect and resonate outwardly, as well as imbuing ourselves with their memory and invoking our very essence with those precious and sacred souls that are now departed from this mortal earthly plain and who now reside in a different place, the space I prefer to call and refer to as 'The Summerlands.'

Forged throughout Time

DIRECTLY DESCENDED OUT of and from the very womb of creation, through the heavy mists of time and delivered to this point, we are all representations and carry within us the very source of all life, the universe and everything that is contained within it.

Guardians and keepers of the richly imbued and woven tapestry that has been stitched with the patterning of life and has been since the dawning of time, as a collective of souls, past and present, we stand here endowed with great powers which have been presented to us and gifted within us by all the spirits that have ever lived.

All that we have and all that we are has been left to us as the most incredible legacy that there is, which will become the very legacy that we in time, pass on to the next generations to come, our children, our grandchildren and so on. The infinite and ever evolving parchments and fabrics of time roll out before us and it is our time now to put our marks upon them and make those generations that are to come, proud of us and what we have achieved, just as we are with those who have gone before us.

The world and the combined societies which we all inhabit and live our daily lives in are a direct attribute, and reminder, of all of those valiant souls that endured and persevered throughout their lives making the most of what they had. Thus making sure we have everything at our disposal which we have today, and often take for granted.

Ground breaking feats and inventions throughout history have all come into play due to chance findings, deep thought and some incredible inventions, all of which we owe immense thanks to our predecessors and Ancestors, without whom, life would be so much different and a lot more difficult.

Since taking those very slow, tentative and arduous first steps of our human evolution, which in itself is nothing short of humbling and miraculous, mankind, in all of its various guises has shown tenacity, cunning, strength, foresight and amazing levels of resilience, being able to endure hardships beyond comprehension and the sheer base guile to adapt to any given situation that arises.

From the water sources that are vital to our very existence, and the many foodstuffs needed to ensure our strength and physical wellbeing and health, to the discovery of sparks, flames and fire, to cook on, protect us and give us lighting and warmth; many of these discoveries ultimately were by chance. Take nothing away from the fact that there has been the understanding and bravery needed to harness many of these elements to aid and assist us in our daily lives. The comprehension and controlling of many of these accomplishments is nothing short of monumental, especially when you imagine how extremely frightening these powers would have seemed millions of years ago, it is incredible to even think about, let alone contemplate, how vulnerable mankind was in the earliest days way back in the aeons of time when nothing was understood and every discovery was literally brand new, like a total awakening of all the senses.

We only have to look at the transport we are freely able to use today and see how it has all come into being. As with the majority of everyday items, we can now ascertain how they have all evolved into the wonders we know, recognise and use today. From what is now fairly primeval in the basic discovery and usage of the very humble wheel, look at how this has formed a constant throughout history, enabling so much of what has happened over time, throughout our history and our lives today. The very invention of the wheel ensured everything from heavy logs, foods and a multitude of vital stocks could be moved around so much easier, imagine the pride and sheer joy when this most basic of tools was discovered and how much easier it would have made people's lives back in the mists of time. This basic attribute would have alleviated so much hardship from these primitive beings and paved the way for the mass movements of goods and utilities that we now have and seemingly take for granted today.

Look at the vital medicines and medical procedures which the majority of us around the world are lucky enough to have easy access to in this day and age. It's barbaric and archaic for us now to rationalise the very thought of death and disease from what we deem now as basic and treatable ailments. Look at the relative ease that sickness's, cuts, abrasions and severe life threatening complaints and conditions can be readily treated now, almost instantly and these discoveries are still ongoing and obviously always will be. The longevity that is abundant in today's society is again a factor of what the ancestors went through and for their part in the most natural and basic of medicinal discoveries.

From the very humble beginnings once again, the chance findings of basic poultices that would have stemmed bleeding, got rid of ulcers and lesions, maybe certain mosses, leafy bundles, right through to the chewing and consumption of natural juices mixed together then drunk or applied, it is these very primitive blends that were sought within the vegetation that would have been abundant within the natural world that these precious spirits, our ancestors would have foraged for, that provided the basic healings that would have been much needed in what was then, a very dangerous and hostile place to live.

Everything that we have and are today, the intricacies right through to the eccentricities, the great and the seemingly absurd; can all be attributed to and find their roots connected to our ancestors perseverance and tenacity to move forward, adapt and seek new ideas which made their lives more bearable and relatively easier with slightly more comfort. This has stood the test of time and everything can be allocated right back to these earliest and most humble of beginnings.

In the world in which we live now and where we have, for the most of us, fairly lavish lifestyles where everything is on tap, accessible and easy, has its foundations firmly rooted in the past. Without the early origins of, what may seem now fairly archaic and antiquated, the majority of the lives we have, live and enjoy would simply not be possible and all these basic recognisable ways of living could never have come into being.

Take nothing away from today's great innovators, scientists and discoverers who constantly working, often behind the scenes, to arrive at new understandings to enhance and better our lives in our society. Yet I have no doubt that they would freely admit that without the groundbreaking pioneers of history providing the very fabric backdrop that designates what we have in our world today, they would not be able to work and further advance those seemingly humble ideas which came into being in the first place. It is from these original concepts that everything we are used to and utilise in our everyday lives have been derived and delivered from.

We only have to look and listen to the multi cultural and diverse number of languages that there are in the world today, yes some of these are relatively recent, yet the base core of vocalised communication, in its multiple guises was voiced and used a long time ago.

Migration of Our Ancestors

FROM THE VERY first moments since our very distant relations started to wonder about where and who they were, an amazing journey has taken place. The first creatures resembling primates who are our long lost and now extinct cousins, have been established clearly as living and surviving on earth as far back as 55 million years ago. Since this arrival, the process has been slow, arduous and nothing short of miraculous. If we take a look now upon mankind's journey to this moment, it is clear to see and comprehend how we have arrived at this point in time within the body vessels which we inhabit. Yet how did we end up travelling and consequently inhabiting all four corners of the globe, from the baron and inhospitable tundra areas, right through to the immensely humid and vegetation rich grasslands and forest regions that reside along the earth's equator?

Effectively, the earth that we live upon is a constantly moving, living and breathing planet. It is self-sufficient, needs no fuel to propel itself and has its own admittedly changeable climates, It is this that aided and enforced our migration from the regions we existed in since our very conception and arrival upon this beautiful world in which we survive, exist and live.

Our migration began around one million years ago, before this our dim and distant relatives had survived and existed within small pockets and communities spread throughout the lands, although the vast majority of all Humans were derived from the African continent and this is the main place where our migration began from. As a living and breathing planet, the earth heats up and cools down. This is normal, yet when it becomes extreme, ice ages happen, volcanoes erupt, and mass devastation can wreak havoc, land masses alter significantly and extremities in temperatures are caused. Hidden within the earth are several layers of crust. This crusting is known as the tectonic plates and it is these plates that hold one of the keys to the earth's stability. This plating is what effectively keeps the happy medium, or balance within the very base structure of our world. In times of normal temperatures rising and falling, these crusts remain relatively stable, yet in times of extreme temperatures, they inevitably move and this can create sudden rises and falls in temperature on the very opposite and extreme ends of the spectrum. When this happens, volcanoes can erupt with such ferocity that their effect can be felt for hundreds, if not thousands of miles. On the opposite side, temperatures can plummet throwing vast lands into what we now call an ice age. Combined within this, the stability of earth is lost, the tectonic plates shift with such force that lands which were once connected can be ripped apart and totally separated, causing immense voids that are often filled by an adjoining sea, therefore a new land mass is created out of what was a larger mass before this shift took place.

The continent which we now know as Africa, which was the greatest landmass at the time and was therefore where the majority of our ancient cousins and Ancestors lived, would have been a very hospitable region in the earliest of times while we were undergoing the very slow process of evolution. Vegetation would have been extremely rich and in abundance and also our thought processes would have still been fairly limited, so the urge to leave and find somewhere more sustainable to live would have been beyond comprehension. Gradually over time this would all change and our base human instinct of survival would play a massive part in the places we migrated to, as did the earth's crusting and tectonic plates shifting, providing us with no alternative apart from enforced migratory journeys of discovery.

Our species, along with all the various species that have contributed to our evolution are now and inevitably always have been creatures of habit. To make such dramatic and often drastic choices of mass exodus tells us that there were no other options available. This can be and is invariably caused by extreme shifts within the earth's interior, causing devastation which results in inhospitable regions where it is almost impossible to survive. Also as in later stages of humanity, warring and massacre have had the same effects on countless numbers of people. Either way migration becomes the only choice and possible hope for survival.

Around 1 million years ago the vast landmass which is Africa was enduring an ice age. It is from this point that we can pinpoint what was to become the migration and exploration to new lands and other continents that our Ancestors embarked upon, simply because the lands they had lived upon were basically totally frozen making life and their very existence almost impossible. Homo erectu, (upright being) was a relatively free-thinking cousin of ours and it is from these early times that they decided to look for new places to settle and live in, escaping what had become a very harsh climate indeed, so the migration out of Africa began.

Human migration, at these early stages of the realisation of ourselves and the world around us, was a very slow and gradual process. Once the first tentative steps had been taken to actually move and look for other places that would have been less harsh and relatively easier to survive in, these people, our most ancient of ancestors were actually stepping into the unknown. They would have had absolutely no idea whatsoever where they were going, what they would find and actually if there really were any other places outside of what they knew. These brave and intrepid souls were embarking on the very first awakenings and discoveries into what was a totally unknown and unchartered world.

Once these precarious and formidable first steps of what would ultimately become mankind's slow dispersal into and around the world began, life would take on a new meaning and all of our levels of consciousness would evolve. Quite simply, the beginning of our awakenings into and around the world would commence, a rebirthing and discovery not only of ourselves, but also of the world around us. From these very humble first steps, our arrival into what can only be called a brave new world was stirring and, step by step, it was about to begin.

Once the first steps of human migration began, we were on a journey that would over many thousands of years ultimately see us venture to every piece of land throughout the world. Due to natural climate changes, which are inevitable, always have been and always will be; this has seen us many times inhabit a land, live and adapt to the surroundings within a specific area, effectively calling it home. Then because of harsh changes, we had to leave simply to ensure our survival. This is significant and shows how resilient we are and always have been as a species, especially in the earliest of times when, if we couldn't adapt to the changes in temperature, we either made the choice to leave and seek new places which were less harsh and more hospitable to our needs, or we died and endangered our race of beings with the possibility of becoming extinct.

The slow migration which would eventually see us inhabiting and thriving the world over was indeed painfully slow. To begin with the migratory generation may well have only moved a few miles from their point of origin. Within this though, new and larger generations were being born, adding significantly to the numbers. Then from these larger communities, the outward spread would increase over the years and subsequently from generation to generation. Our migration from, and out of, Africa around one million years ago was now underway and would slowly pick up pace, seeing us gradually inhabit and thrive within various parts of all continents over many thousands of years.

Around 150,000 years ago, our species, Homo sapiens, appear to have returned once again to the continent of Africa, the land of our origin. They had slowly dispersed and now journeyed back in large numbers. To return to our homelands is what we see now as almost instinctual. Re-visiting the place of our birth, would have been a base core yearning for our Ancestors, it would have been a necessity simply because of inhospitable climates, ice ages and such like in the new areas they had spread to. Returning once again to Africa would have endorsed our survival and it was within Africa that we would remain through this enforced return, for around 70,000 years.

As recently as 80,000 years ago our ancestors migrated once again, although this time, our numbers were far larger. The journey we embarked upon once again would have been relatively quicker, although not in comparison to today's time scale. With each passing generation, an imprint of social learning, adaptability, creation and memory, along with natural survival instincts were all passed down through the hereditary lineage.

It is all these past experiences, trials and how to overcome obstacles, that are endorsed upon our very DNA and core being. Nowadays, we know that we inherit wisdom, knowledge and an immeasurable amount of various traits from our parents and forefathers. It would have been at around this time of 80,000 years ago that we can truly see this inherited learning starting to show within our ancient ancestors.

The sheer scale, enforced or not, of this mass exodus is nothing short of incredible and absolutely humbling. It is nothing to us to drive a few hundred miles a day, or to climb onboard a plane and jet half way around the world. We know what is waiting for us; a place to stay, food to eat and everything that we are accustomed to. Imagine though, having to leave simply because the lands that have birthed and nourished you and your family for countless generations are now inhospitable and have become baron and frozen over. The understandings and ingenuity needed to survive within these climates was way beyond our capabilities at that time. We, as a race, were not adapted enough to endure and live within these desperate times on such a barren landscape. In time, we would learn to adapt. Not in those times though when, as a species, we were still relatively new to, not only living, but also to the seemingly ever changing world around us within which we were almost fighting day to day with the elements and still attempting to eke out a constant and comfortable way of life.

The larger numbers of these early people was growing all the time and this period of human migration would see us move out of Africa and gradually expand across what we now know as the continent of Asia, also covering parts of Europe (often referred to nowadays as Eurasia, a culmination of both).

As we ventured and migrated out of our homeland of Africa

once again, we would have inevitably had learned a vast number of skills. From hunting and cooking to gaining knowledge of plants that were edible. Also, communication would have improved, all of which helped greatly with survival. So this time we were much better equipped, although this does not detract at all from what would have still been a very intimidating time, extremely unsettling, arduous and life threatening, simply because, once again, we were venturing into and exploring new lands and heading into new territory.

During this time, slowly and surely our distant Ancestors travelled further and further into and across what we now call Europe: Spain, Italy and Germany mainly. There is strong evidence that substantiates this. Along with parts of Eurasia as well: Russia, Belarus, Kazakhstan and the Baltic regions. Some of these areas had been inhabited before this period, now though, larger numbers were arriving and once again settling down and surviving there.

Around the time of approximately 40,000–80,000 years ago homo sapiens (or humans), our direct ancestors were expanding in vast numbers, enough to build up close communities and village settlements throughout large areas of different continents and countries of which we are all aware of today. It is also around the time of 40,000 years ago when we were still continuing to expand and grow in numbers that saw our ever growing population spread further into unsettled parts of Europe and also reaching into and arriving at undiscovered parts of modern day countries like Italy and Spain. It is around this period in history that we discovered we were not alone, ultimately venturing into unchartered areas and regions, we encountered new people, a race seemingly very different to our own; we came face to face with the Neanderthals.

Around the time of 40,000 years ago, Europe was very different from what we know it as today. It was very cold and vast expanses of it were frozen; a very formidable place indeed. The ever mounting numbers of Homo sapiens were now encroaching into countries that seemed inhospitable for many previous generations. Now though, equipped with greater numbers, effective knowledge of survival, hunting and clothing, our Ancestors had a way of coping in what was still an extremely tough environment in which to live.

Coming face to face with the neanderthals at this time would have been very intimidating indeed and also for the neanderthals as well. Effectively, two very different species, yet similar in many ways, now came into direct contact. For what would have been the first time since mankind first started to venture and migrate, these two types of being came face to face; a very daunting prospect for both species.

Neanderthals were very hardy and resilient beings. There is evidence to show that they had been living across much of Europe, inhabiting the lands from Siberia through to Spain, for approximately 250,000 years. Highly skilled hunters who had learnt to use the ever changing environments of that time to their advantage.

As part of the chain that forms human beings, the neanderthals are a direct cousin of ours and new technology and science has shown that many of us carry neanderthal genes within our DNA. Bone and skull fragments that have been unearthed and discovered have been painstakingly pieced together and it is from these that we are able to show the variations of ourselves and between our neanderthal cousins.

Heavy ridged brows were a very significant variation within these beings who were thicker set in stature. A larger brain is evident as well as is the more muscular build which can be seen in skeletal build-ups and images created from pieces that have been discovered over time.

Having inhabited parts of Europe for around 250,000 years, our distant neanderthal cousins would have had a very resilient nature. The ever changing landscapes would have been relatively inhospitable, yet here they had remained and survived for many tens of thousands of years. Their physicality had adapted to their surroundings, they had learnt how to hunt and what to hunt for maximum efficiency and well being which all culminates into the evolution of them as a species, albeit linked to us and from where we ultimately have arrived from through the chain of beings who have played a part in our conception. To this day some of us carry them within our very core and base make up as part of our DNA structure.

Imagine the first meeting of these two. Surely fear and dread would have been felt and resonated outwardly from both parties. For all concerned, they had been living and surviving as best and efficiently as they could, not knowing there were others inhabiting the often unforgiving and very treacherous lands they called home. Then seemingly out of nowhere, others arrived, looking similar, yet very different in appearance. We can only imagine as to what happened when both parties encountered one another. It is apparent that eventually and over many years, as a species of their own, neanderthals became extinct. Although their lineage remains within many of us to this day, proving that through and over time, Homo sapiens and neanderthals bred together through several generations and over many years.

With the obviously larger brains and stronger stature that shaped the neanderthals, why did they fade away and become extinct as a singular species and not homo sapiens? They were obviously better adapted to living in these tougher climates than we were, they had survived in barren and freezing landscapes for 250,000 years, so what happened and why aren't we all neanderthals now instead of homo sapiens?

Slowly and over many years, we built up larger numbers of our group and species, obviously because there were more of us to begin with and with the ever growing population of us, Homo sapiens, we effectively needed more and more lands to build our communities upon. This community building could help to explain and be a key factor in our survival. As we spread throughout Europe approximately 40,000 years ago, we interacted with one another and this has been clear throughout history. Communities talk, we share similar traits, beliefs and to maintain this balance we have to share and keep the lines of communication open. As we advanced, these groups, communities and family numbers grew, we spread further When times were tough, we aided one another.

In comparison neanderthals who had lived across Europe for many, many generations, appear to have been fairly solitary and didn't live within larger groups as we did. Discoveries found from that time make it clear that we were both capable of hunting and surviving. So once we started to expand with our ever growing numbers, it does become apparent that they started to retreat as their numbers lessened considerably. If we then look at how both different yet similar species interacted, which caused sexual breeding we can see that because of our far superior and greater numbers it seems clear that eventually the neanderthal species became very diluted and eventually extinct, apart from within some homo sapiens as a part of their base molecular build-up and DNA.

Beyond any shadow of a doubt, we have all, in much majestic splendour and beauty descended and originated from Africa. This was where proto-humans evolved into homo sapiens and this is where from a very small pocket of community, we can all trace our inception and arrival into becoming the human beings which we are all today. Over many millennia, our very ancient and first ancestors battled against harsh environments, endured catastrophic climate changes, ferocious animals and would have lost many numbers. Through good fortune, determination and utter resilience, we overcame many adversities and trials and all this while we were still finding our way into and around being human and working out how to actually fit in to the world in which we were living. An unsubstantiated time of peril, endurance and miracles have led us to this point in time and it is only when we think about the journey that was first undertaken by these most sacred of souls that we can actually start to ascertain how extreme the journey has been to get here in the recognisable bodily forms in which we all inhabit.

Once our distant ancestors arrived in Europe from Africa, many changes to our physicality were still taking shape and subtly being formed. Effectively, we were a work in progress and this has always been the way; a slow and gradual evolution as a way of adapting and fitting into our surroundings.

The most noticeable change, once we had been in Europe for many generations, were our colouration, or skin pigmentation. Darker skin is essential to us if we reside in and are from Africa, simply because it protects us from the intense and unforgiving sun which, if we did not have this protection would simply burn us. This was equally apparent then as much as it is nowadays.

After many generations and several millennia of not living in Africa and inhabiting the cooler continent of Europe, we would have gradually lightened up on the skin colouration which we had and one highly likely answer to this is because after living without the intensity of the sun and also enduring vastly colder climates, we naturally started to lack and lose a lot of the Vitamin D which is mainly given to us and absorbed naturally by our bodies from the sun.

Evidence found that collaborates our arrival in Europe around 40,000 years ago has been recently discovered. In 2002 in Romania hundreds of separate skull fragments were discovered in a cave and after some intense and very laborious piecing together, an almost whole skull was formed. This skull underwent many tests and this very skull gives us conclusive evidential proof that Homo sapiens did indeed inhabit and live in Europe at around the time of 40,000 years ago. Although, thanks to this finding and undoubtedly over time there will be many others, we now know definitively that we, as a species, lived and thrived throughout vast parts of the continent of Europe at that time.

At around 24,000 years ago, the U.K. and Europe was in the grip of what is the most recent ice age. The lands were totally devoid of lush vegetation and vast swathes of this land were effectively barren. This ice age had lasted across many countries for thousands and thousands of years. Although, with glaciers melting and the subsequent warming of the planet, places did thaw out, allowing plants and trees to grow in different areas from time to time, which then provided some food and it became a slightly less harsh environment to live in. It was this ice age melt of around 18,000 years ago that would effectively grant us passage across to what we now know as the U.S. and the Americas.

The inhabitants and communities that lived across Europe and the U.K. during the last ice age had learnt how to survive in these very hostile conditions; we did not migrate as we had done many generations before. Learning to adapt and with new and improved methods of hunting, utilising the whole of the animals that had been killed, not just for food but also for clothing and bedding, it is these small steps that helped and aided us immensely. These relatively small adaptations enabled us to insulate ourselves properly against the frozen lands and biting winds that were everywhere during this time.

For the relatively new race of Europeans that were now living during this period, the journey into caves was groundbreaking. Once inside and deep within a cave structure, you escape the intensity of the prevailing weather that is constant outside. A constant temperature of around 4 degrees Celsius is maintained and that is before the introduction of fire which helped with heat, lighting and warding off dangerous animals and would be attackers. Plus the fire provided the way to cook food and also brought the community together, giving inspiration and a focal point as well as protection and warmth, inwardly from the foods cooked and outwardly to warm and dry us from the heat that the flames gave.

Living within caves and the adjoining systems within them was not a new concept and evidence shows us that caves had been used before. However, for the new European beings, this was a very innovative idea, simply because our Ancestors who decided to venture and spread out across these lands were the very first of our race to reside here.

There have been many finds in caves within the U.K. and across Europe; bone fragments and almost whole skeletons, assorted pottery, jewellery and even musical instruments. Along with stunningly intricate cave paintings and etchings that adorn the walls. Many of these incredible findings that have been unearthed so far have been aged and dated. All the corresponding data found shows us that it is all from this period, around 20,000 years ago.

Living in these parts at this time would have been incredibly harsh and every day would have been a constant battle for survival. Not only would these arctic type lands and weather patterns wipe out some of the animals, also these ferocious and unforgiving natural elements of weather would have undoubtedly been responsible for killing off many of these ancient souls who would have been ravaged by the relentless ice and freezing temperatures that prevailed. The only escape being was inside the caves that now sheltered them and became their homes.

By then larger numbers and connecting communities would have been in place and this would have been a key part in our survival around that time. The greater the numbers you have, the greater the communication, within which many various ideas are put forward, which is always good. There is strength in numbers, this much is clear and it would have been so apparent at those times and proved vital to their existence.

Ravaged and almost annihilated by the harsh and very extreme conditions, we can see true perseverance and tenacity to battle through and overcome whatever was thrown at us by the elements within an almost totally void landscape. Within the endurance and utmost resilience needed to simply get through each day, these sacred people used the time, to paint and etch beautiful and very intricate pictures on the walls of the caves which they called home. Flutes carved out of bones and animal horn have been found also dating back to those times within some of the caves. Which again goes to show that even during catastrophic and life threatening times of early man upon these lands, music would have been played and enjoyed by the communities and different settlements throughout.

Playing music, painting on cave walls and enjoying life at the end of a gruelling day just shows us how far mankind had come.

From the very earliest of times, a small group of homo sapiens that lived in Africa, where we are all from, had started to slowly increase in numbers, and then started to venture out and explore the wider world around. The first journeys of Man were incredibly tough and, at every turn, they were often beaten back and had no other option but to return from where they had come. In these most humble of beginnings, we were not equipped at all to endure, neither could we adapt.

The period of time from 20,000–40,000 years ago is the most fundamentally important time in the history of civilisation, coming to and inhabiting large swathes of Europe and the U.K. Having survived an ice age and endured the harsh battles with the elements, mankind had shown his strength and resilience. Within all of this, obviously having lost many members of various communities throughout this time, they had still managed (with all the odds unfavourably stacked against them) to come through it all intact and more so, their numbers had sustained substantially enough to continue producing the next generation.

The period in our history of approximately 18,000 years ago saw the last ice age starting to dissipate and melt away, although it would take thousands of years to fully retreat. Even now, there are residual glaciers and heavy snow coverings that still remain and serve as constant reminders of this very different and much harsher world than the majority of us live in today.

Life would have carried on as it had done over subsequent generations and would continue to do so, pretty much in the same way as it had. Constantly though, numbers were building and growing all the time. It is this continuation and strengthening within numbers that had seen us migrate and reach this point where communities had been built and villages assembled throughout much of the world we had explored since originally leaving our African homelands as a very small band of pioneers and migrants looking to broaden our horizons almost a million years beforehand.

From around 15,000 years ago the numbers of our Ancestors inhabiting Europe had expanded enough for us to want to explore and venture out even further. This has always been the case since our inception upon this planet way back in the mists of time. Greater numbers and human curiosity now made this happen and it is from 15,000 years ago, that we were to venture into the Americas and slowly spread over and through the vast expanses of lands that there are within that enormous continent.

The Neolithic period or late Stone Age is the period in our history that started in and around 17,000 and lasted until approximately 2,000 years BCE. Thought to have its origins within the Middle East and slowly stretching out to many parts of the world, it is this time that saw many transformational changes across the spectrums of how we lived and worked. Often referred to as a revolution it is during this time that would see us totally transform from relatively simple beings in the way we lived and worked and evolve into quite complex beings that managed and worked the land. From this time we moved away from the constant hunting with fairly basic tools, new discoveries were being made all the time and it is then that we made the conscious decision to work and farm the lands.

This is a monumental leap forward and once again shows us how adept and knowledgeable we had become. Our levels of understanding and our comprehension of the natural world around us had increased to such a level that we decided to make the move away from merely being opportunistic hunters who killed simply because we needed sustenance. We were now turning to farming and agriculture of the lands which would ensure our survival and longevity for countless generations to come. It is from these decisions made many thousands of years ago that we continue to live and farm to this day.

The advancements in natural farming, planting and harvesting during this time explains the sheer diversity in logical reasoning and complex long term planning and is a milestone in just how far we had come to get to this point. Our ancestors truly were becoming advanced and were more higher thinking than ever before. It has to be this move into farming and having the depth of comprehension that virtually guaranteed that we would continue to grow in numbers, our health would improve and we would continue the expansion across the world.

Our most sacred and ancient of ancestors had seen and been witness to so much including the migrations back and forth, the hostility of the world around them and the freezing temperatures, the blazing heat, starvation and disease. All of this just as they were coming to terms and finding their feet.

We all stand here today as tributes to these beautiful souls. Their immense suffering, the totally transient lives they would have had to endure for countless years, the confusion, total bewilderment and devastating losses they went through, yet they finally prevailed and set out the benchmark and understanding, which they gifted to us in their legacies. It is from this template, etched way back in time, that they effectively started to understand the world around them in close proximity and enough to work with it. They stood the test of time, procuring their existence which in turn endorsed our survival and the continuation of the homo sapiens species as we now know and appreciate today.

Life continued for thousands of years. Our ancestors farmed the lands and tended to their crops. From this move into agricultural knowledge and utilisation of the lands came strength and fortitude. Larger communities sprung up with greater numbers in population. This expanding way of farming ensured much better health, longer life spans and continued understandings of how to sustain one another. Thriving villages were now shifting across the lands and this way of life rapidly spread across different continents as numbers grew, then people moved. It continued in this way and effectively has done so ever since.

With newer discoveries and ideas coming to fruition over time, it wasn't long until these new findings and concepts were assisting us greatly in our day to day lives. This was paramount once again at around 4,000 years ago when we moved into what we now know and refer to as the Bronze Age. Metal was now a main part of how we could farm, and along with many other uses. This discovery of metal, and how to use it, strengthened our way of being once again. This allowed us to create a wider array of tools and from this, other ideas came about as they always do.

We moved into the Iron Age about 2,500–3,000 years ago, this once again proved to be a highly significant step forward and the process of extracting and purifying iron ore from the ground, then heating and shaping of it into tools, basic machinery and a wide array of other implements, was a highly innovative idea and discovery. After several years and generations getting used to this new found, malleable and highly tough discovery of iron, we really moved forward once again.

With the innovation and understanding of this newly discovered metal and the working and shaping of it, agriculture and localised farming underwent a huge change. More land could now be farmed, larger areas could be maintained without as much labour. This shows us, yet again, that greater numbers of people and inhabitants of larger communities could (barring any natural disasters that may occur) farm the lands, harvest the crops and almost guarantee the survival of whole villages and settlements.

This ever expanding growth in population was once again vital for our ancestor's survival and after having gone through so much, as each generation would have done, they must have felt as if most of the hard times were behind them. During the iron age ultimately came another expansion. This expansion would have been spreading throughout the known and inhabited world at the time, simply due to farming methods, basic technologies and healthier people. It was at this time that the Celtic expansion took place and this saw greater parts of Western Europe and larger parts of the British Isles becoming populated with what were the ever growing and more advanced people that had succeeded and thrived throughout the previously inhabited lands.

Between the phases of time around 2,000–1,500 years ago the ever extensive shift and populating as a necessity of farming moved ever forward and throughout the world as was known at the time. Lands were being cultivated more extensively than ever before. This arable scene could now be viewed as widespread across Europe and this bought along much larger colonies of people with it. To this day, many of the areas which are now set aside for arable crop rotation are lands which were tilled and planted from these earliest steps into farming productivity.

Once farming had taken off completely, as people realised the importance of sustainable farming (which included the planting, maintaining, harvesting and long term storage of all the crops) the link was truly made with the significant importance of sustaining the people and assuring they were kept alive. This really was a momentous breakthrough in the long term survival of humans as a race. Simply because by this time we had spread around most of the world and it is by these early and fairly primitive (by today's standards of agricultural farming that we have managed to expand and successfully migrate to the far flung corners of the world and carve out our survival and an income at the same time.

Across various lands and different areas around the world, migration has been happening since the dawn of time, that much is clear. It is as common today as it has been throughout history. There have been, and sadly there still are, periods of unrest along and through parts of the world. This can bring on enforced migration, which is not often today due to severe weather changes but has been brought about by wars and invasion by other foreign peoples. Again this is a sad fact and one that is not new at all.

At around 1,200 years ago, the U.K. and large areas of Europe came under attack and were invaded by people from the North. The Vikings from Scandinavia landed upon our shores and wreaked havoc among the people. After raiding these lands and parts of Europe they decided eventually to settle down and forge a life for themselves across France, Ireland, Scotland and England. If we look down through our lineage and DNA today with the aid of medical science, we can clearly see that these invasions started off terrifyingly for our ancestors who were invaded at the time. Eventually though we learnt to live alongside the intruders to the point where interbreeding played a huge part in the further evolution of our identities and the very genes that form who we are today.

Reflections

TO GAZE BACK and reflect upon the journey that our ancestors embarked upon around one million years ago, when they took the very first tentative step upon what was going to become the path of human migration, is simply miraculous. These very first precarious, naïve footprints were the beginning of our species' journey which would eventually see us cross all seven continents, discover, visit and revisit many times, totally unchartered, beautiful, barren, void and wondrous places. As with any new beginning and embarkation of any new odyssey which we pursue and wish to start out upon, it begins with the very first step, from that point it has begun. Nowadays whenever we travel somewhere, we are normally fully aware of where we are heading to and what we will find, more or less, when we reach our destination.

One million years ago, when the migration of our human race came into being, our ancestors did not have the luxury of knowing what lay before them, what they may encounter, where they were actually going, or heading to or even if there was anything past the area they were accustomed to.

When we think about early pioneers and individuals who have left to explore new areas, we often view them as extremely brave and resilient people who are very driven and feel the need to take themselves off on an expedition, exploring new heights to hopefully conquer what has not been achieved before. These journeys are all good and show a continuation of our inner curiosity, utter determination, doggedness and strength of the human spirit, all of which undoubtedly stems from these earliest travellers and lone pioneers of our race.

Nowadays, any new journey we undertake is relatively easy. Radio communications are in abundance now, lightweight warm clothing, high energy foods and drinks and portable shelters which can be easily obtained and carried. So as brilliant and remarkable as these feats of endurance are, and I take nothing away from them at all, there is no comparison to the first pioneers and those who migrated out of Africa in our earliest days.

This journey that we started out upon was literally the birthing of man into and around the world. From our most humble of beginnings and our very slow and gradual evolution from early and very primitive primate species, the interaction with other beings, saw us shaped into the race we recognise and all stand as today, the bastions and legacies of these first stirrings. This moment one million years ago was the point at which we were to emerge from, like another birthing. Only this was to be the introduction of human beings that would eventually see us venture into totally unknown lands, charter all seven continents and succeed on the quest which we were inevitably placed here to fulfil.

To reflect upon this brings us closer with an intricate under-standing as to how and what they were actually stepping into. These early beings, our ancestors were not equipped at all for the journey they were just about to undertake. Also they had no idea of the great results that would come from those first steps.

Within our modern minds and rational thinking, we have the luxury of being able to think abstractly and logically and work out ideas and plans which we may want to put into action. This comes from knowledge and we have that in abundance, both within us (which is the font that links us to the universe and is called the collective unconsciousness), plus we have an immeasurable amount of physical resources to draw ideas and solutions from. Imagine not having that luxury and literally everything that you attempted to undertake and any ideas you may have were coming to you as brand new and never before thought of plans or ideas. This was literally the beginning of the collective unconscious, the infinite pool that links all life and creation together.

To reflect and ponder on this is one of the most important ways in which we can get a stance on not only the physical undertakings of just what these earliest people had to endure, but also the total comprehension of what an absolutely momentous path lay ahead of them and every single action they decided to follow through and act out. These people were literally like a computer without a hard drive or memory, nothing had been stored and there was nothing to search for, a huge empty void basically, so anything that became stored was being played out for the very first time. Obviously the base instincts were there, the need to eat, drink and sleep, apart from that though, there was literally nothing. That was all waiting to be collected and installed and this was the beginning of that journey of mental stimulation and mindfulness, something which we all have today.

Africa the lands of our arrival and evolution into humans had cradled us in the very young and formative years. It had provided sustenance and allowed us to gradually awaken into our physical selves. Our homelands had given us the nurture we needed, just as a mother caresses and encourages their small children to take their first steps, in this instance though, mans first steps were going to be into what was a very different, harsh and totally unknown world. From these most basic of beginnings, we were not equipped at all and were devoid of the physicality to endure, the mental capacity to overcome and the spirituality that gives us hope and belief.

It is almost impossible to imagine just what was going through their minds as they set off on the path that was to irrevocably become the most arduous and fascinating journey ever undertaken. The accompanying factual tales of discovery are the greatest story ever told.

To glance back on the evolution and migration of our race as human beings is totally awe inspiring. As with any given situation, hindsight is a wonderful tool. To recollect just what went on, what happened and the dogged tenacity that came into being at times of extreme and often brutal hardship, is mesmerising. Again, this shows us the luxury of having hindsight, something that these sacred souls were not endowed with.

As with any new start and beginning, the human race of beings came about very slowly and extremely tentatively, unsure and unstable within our own being, naïve to the world around us and so vulnerable to the whole of creation that was spread out and laid before us.

Like the most sublime and gentlest of ripples that reach out and then slowly dissipate across the calmest of water; our first venturing into the world mirrored the calm waters. We reached out into the wilderness, stretched as far as we could, then dissipated and at first we retreated back to Africa, the womb and heartbeat of our existence and creation. Slowly and surely, we started to gather momentum and accrued larger numbers which ensured more strength in what was our most fragile of beginnings.

As our numbers from generation to generation grew, so did our physical, mental and spiritual awareness. Admittedly this took many hundreds of thousands of years, which is to be expected, yet eventually we became much stronger, as would be expected. This is clearly apparent both within our own being and the assuredness that naturally comes from being part of a larger group of people, especially at this most vulnerable of times when we began awakening together as a community and tribe.

Upon the upsurge of our numbers and the human race as a whole, we began to form smaller pockets and communities throughout the hospitable and inhabitable lands we reached into. Although within these groups, we were also in communication with the next community, which is shown and clear through discoveries made over time throughout our history. This has been a key point in our survival and shows us now that communication is pivotal for any existence and partnership to remain open and strong. Not only is this clear to see for mankind, we only have to look to the way animals exist and communicate amongst themselves to see how they manage to survive and strengthen their numbers through channels of communication.

Eventually, and over many generations, our numbers had substantially grown enough to allow us (along with shared and collected knowledge, which again is vital to our existence) to spread into many parts of what we now know as the recognised and modern world. From the most humble of origins, we had become and evolved into a huge collective, expanding constantly. Like a continual rippling correlation of beings, a vast living and breathing collective, gathering pace constantly, spreading our seeds and reaching out to new and undiscovered lands.

The reflection into the past and the sheer awe inspiring realisation of just how we arrived and came into being is nothing short of fantastic. The gradual process of our awakening from the first stirrings through to the growth in numbers, the first migration we embarked upon, the retreat, the growth again and then the journey that would see us cross huge voids and waters.

As we gaze back with awe and wonderment upon this incredible story, which provides the factual backdrop and is how we got to this point, what we are effectively doing is unpicking the very threads of our history. In doing so, we are discovering a wealth of ancestry, which in turn, brings us closer and closer to our very own ancestors, our heritage and our lineage.

It is only when we look at the bigger picture, and that is evident with any subject or situation, that we can then truly see and start to comprehend the inner and most intricate pieces of the puzzle and the very dynamics that everything has arisen from and is built upon.

Reflection and hindsight are very similar and once we take the time to cast our minds back and venture into the past, then we become aware of how everything has fallen into place and none of it is by accident, it's because it is all supposed to happen as it has done. From this stance, we can see the accumulation of all the finer workings and properties that have all played a part in the linking and subsequent formation of individual pieces that when placed together, all correspond and link up to create the larger picture that has been painted for us all to see now in all of its glory.

Stepping stones of time, each one placed carefully, which then allows the next one to be cast and so on. It is only now that it has become possible, with the aid of understanding and ageing discoveries made with the new concepts of scientific research, that we are able to literally bring the past to life and venture into the vast world that was laid out before these most sacred of souls who have now become, and will always remain, our ancestors and the forerunners of the journey of all human life.

Conclusion

SINCE OUR MOST vulnerable state of awareness and arrival onto this planet, we have as a species been on the most amazing of journeys. A constant awakening of our state of being, our perceptions and growth, physically, mentally and spiritually. Awareness of who and what we are and the ever changing environments in which we have existed and overcome obstacles and reached an understanding of the planet shows the total resilience of our species. We are far more adaptive than any other species alive, we can constantly change, grow and evolve and this shows in the foods we have found available within and across the continents which we have continued to expand and surge across. Our intuitive state and our comprehension shows we have become equipped on all of our levels to have the stamina and fortitude to not only go through, but also to overcome and survive, any situation that has arisen or befallen us.

To learn not only to adapt, yet also to live in a sustainable manner throughout the world in all of the varying climates and the associated adversities associated with these is a true testimony to just how evolved we have ultimately become and stands as a true benchmark to those most earliest of pioneers of our species who constantly pressed forwards beyond the boundaries and very limitations of what was to be expected. These brave souls laid the foundations for all of our lives and ensured that we would ultimately survive in all of our ethnicities, groups and communities across what we now perceive and refer to as the modern world.

CONCLUSION

The backdrop of our lineage was formed many countless generations ago and within this, we now have the references to look back upon and absorb lessons from. Our journey has not been easy, against the hostile and very harsh world we suddenly found ourselves a part of. To begin with, we languished and suffered much torment, yet we stood resolute. We continued again and again and slowly from that we became aware of ourselves and the surroundings we lived side by side within.

We owe so much to these most ancient beings who never gave up. We need to remember and hold them all in high regard within our thoughts and actions. These souls were the forerunners and bringers of what we have now, what has come into fruition and being. They must not be forgotten for, if that happens, we will fail and stagnate.

As our understandings within science move on and new discoveries come to light, undoubtedly there will be new additions to the comprehensions of exactly where we have come from and the exact processional routes will vary on our migratory routes, that is all par for the course and can only help and assist us in our understandings of the bigger picture of our emergence into the lives we have and enjoy around the world today.

Acceptance and allowing new discoveries and scientific breakthroughs to enhance and broaden our understandings is imperative and this can be seen throughout the world and history. In an age where we are uncovering so much that has remained hidden until now just shows us that we are ready for these massive changes. If we were not ready and viably equipped, they would not be being revealed to us.

An infinite number of interpretations can be placed, and often are, on any given topic and subject, these can be deemed as misplaced and sometimes just dismissed totally. We are now at the point where we know that anything is not only possible, yet highly likely as well, so dismissal is often out of the question.

We have conquered lands, countries and all seven continents within our time here. We have journeyed to the deepest oceans and are now exploring not only our world, yet also other planets that are laid before and around us.

We are living in the greatest of times and ages and we have no limitations, only those that we place upon ourselves. Anything is possible and it is all because of our ancestors and ancestry as a whole and as a collective. They gave us this life and all of the very decadent and lavish lifestyles with which many of us around the world now have the luxury of enjoying today.

The slight variations in our perception of where we came from will inevitably change as time moves on, it always does. The culmination of all that we have though, is a direct link to all of those who broke boundaries and started this amazing journey and evolution of our species that is the human race. That much will not change and we should once again be immensely proud of all of these souls, from the most primeval of ancient beings right through to the most recent of ancestors. We should also be proud of ourselves, not only for what we have done, but also for what we are now doing and will continue to do.

Many thanks for taking the time and energy to read my words contained within this book. If you would like to contact me for any reason, please feel free to do so via my website johnawen. com

I wish you all much love on your journey through life.

Many thanks
John Awen